WHAT HAPPENS NEXT?

happy birthday
to my friend.

I love you so

D1457032

SpT · 13

Iowa and the Midwest Experience

SERIES EDITOR

William B. Friedricks
Iowa History Center at Simpson College

Also by Douglas Bauer

FICTION

Dexterity

The Very Air

The Book of Famous Iowans

NONFICTION

Prairie City, Iowa: Three Seasons at Home

The Stuff of Fiction: Advice on Craft

AS EDITOR

Prime Times: Writers on Their Favorite TV Shows

Death by Pad Thai and Other Unforgettable Meals

WHAT
HAPPENS
NEXT?

჻

Matters of Life and Death
Douglas Bauer

UNIVERSITY OF IOWA PRESS
IOWA CITY

University of Iowa Press, Iowa City 52242
Copyright © 2013 by Douglas Bauer
www.uiowapress.org
Printed in the United States of America
Design by Sara T. Sauers

The University of Iowa Press gratefully acknowledges
Humanities Iowa for its generous support of the Iowa and
the Midwest Experience series.

The University of Iowa Press is a member of Green Press
Initiative and is committed to preserving natural resources.

Printed on acid-free paper

LCCN: 2013934854
ISBN-13: 978-1-60938-183-7
ISBN-10: 1-60938-183-1

For Bob

The end of all our exploring
Will be to arrive where we started
And know the place for the first time.
—T. S. ELIOT, "Little Gidding"

CONTENTS ॐ

ACKNOWLEDGMENTS

"Here We Were at Exactly This Moment" appeared in *Agni*. "Iowa Wine," "The Life He Left Her," and a section of "What We Hunger For" appeared in *Tin House* in slightly different forms. "Tenacity" appeared in *The Massachusetts Review*. A section of "What Was Served" will appear in *Fried Walleye and Cherry Pie: Midwestern Writers on Food*, University of Nebraska Press, 2013.

Thanks go to the National Endowment for the Arts for a fellowship that aided in the writing of this book. Great thanks go as well to Henry Dunow, Dr. Richard Q. Ford, Bill Friedricks, Phillip Lopate, Alice Mattison, Dr. Elizabeth Matzkin, Fiona McCrae, Sue Miller, and Jane Rosenman for their advice and support. And I'm especially indebted to Dr. Peter Rapoza.

INTRODUCTION

IN MY EARLY SIXTIES, and still extraordinarily lucky in my health, I became aware that three key and quite disparate parts of me were showing common signs of wear. It was as if they'd colluded in a devilish partnership to simultaneously launch the beginning mischief of age. First, the cataracts that had long been ripening in both eyes had reached the stage where they needed to be removed. In addition, I'd been feeling my heart begin now and then to beat too rapidly for no reason I could trace. And finally, my arthritic left knee, a problem for decades, most of its cartilage surgically removed when I was twenty-one, was suddenly much crankier—stiffer and more painful—than it had ever been.

So I scheduled a month of appointments and tests and, for the cataracts, routine surgical procedures. I organized everything into a quick, convenient cluster because I was going to be away from home for some months. But also, looking back, I see myself irrationally imagining that if I attended to these matters in a wholesale sweep, it would be as if I were doing away with the evidence that age had found me and settled in to stay.

Arranging this calendar, I had no suspicion that the push of narrative, the stuff of story, was in it.

But I had no suspicion either that my mother would die on the morning of that calendar's first day.

She was a few months shy of eighty-seven and she was naturally, but no more than naturally, frail. She had not been failing, and I found that the surprise of her death brought mood and meaning to days I'd been viewing as nothing more profound than some busy weeks of medical maintenance. But in the wake of her dying I felt myself inside a life of uncanny design, one marked by the dual calendars of her aging and passing and the suddenly heightened sense of my own mortality.

My mind turned repeatedly to thoughts of her, as of course it would. Most often, I thought about her and my father's confounding marriage—its early excitement, its subsequent years of anger and frustration, its brooding culmination, its baffling coda of her first affection's return.

As for me, my body's ordinary maladies became a kind of mental and emotional GPS, freeing my thoughts to relevantly meander, encouraging them to pertinently stray, absent any fear of getting lost. Indeed, there was no lost to get. Losing my way was my scheme for finding it, and my mind wandered among matters and memories—of life and death, of my present and my past, of my childhood place and how much of it has inevitably stayed with me and in me.

This book is the result, a narrative of connected essays. It can be entered at any point, for each piece was written to stand on its own. Or, and I think preferable, it can be read from start to finish, since it's organized to move along with a sense of the tale gathering and building—with very occasional overlap—from beginning to end. The end, that is, of my story so far; not yet, I'm here and pleased to say, the end of me.

WHAT
HAPPENS
NEXT?

HERE WE WERE AT
EXACTLY THIS MOMENT

࿊

THE SUNNY BOSTON WINTER SHONE THROUGH THE WALL of windows, casting us in a warm and welcoming morning light. And the sunlight's disposition was the room's in general, thanks to the nurses moving quickly about like focused, happy hosts. At the moment they were happily hosting two other patients besides myself, the three of us here for cataract surgeries. We were sitting comfortably in something like settees that fold down flat, when your name reaches the top of the list on a large overhead monitor that suggests an airport arrival-and-departure screen—if only airports functioned with such brisk efficiency.

I was partly attentive to the movement all around me and especially to the banter among the nurses and staff, overlapping like chatter in an Altman scene. But my mind was mostly fixed on the conversation I'd had an hour ago with my younger brother, Bob, my only sibling, who was calling from his car in Newton, Iowa, where the sun was just then rising and putting a glaze on the crusted snow and where the temperature was uninhabitably below zero. He was sitting in the otherwise empty parking lot of the hospital where our mother had been a patient for a week.

His cell phone had wakened him on her couch; it was where he always chose to sleep when he drove from St. Louis to visit her in Iowa. Answering, he heard a nurse saying that Mom had had "a pretty bad night" and that he might want to get to the hospital as quickly as he could, a distance of roughly twelve miles from her apartment in the tiny village of Prairie City.

Calling from the parking lot, he said to me, "I haven't gone in yet. I wanted to tell you what was happening." He knew I was scheduled for surgery that morning and he'd timed his call for the hour before I left the house, factoring in the difference between Midwest and East Coast clocks.

We agreed we'd talk again at noon, when I'd returned from the procedure and the drugs had lifted and I would be, I hoped, lucid enough for conversation. He wished me luck, I wished him the same, and I hung up feeling an inseparable layering of guilt and relief and guilt for feeling relief, that he was out there, with her, and I was not.

He'd made the six-and-a-half-hour drive after getting word that she'd fallen again, not as she had five months before when she'd lost her balance while fixing her early supper on a hot August evening and broken her left hip as she hit the kitchen floor. This time she'd fallen outdoors, slipping on the ice as she stepped from her car after driving four blocks from her apartment to the local grocery on the town square.

The Midwest winter had been epically severe. Preposterous extremes of snow and cold had completely stopped the days, sometimes several in a row. Certainly, it had kept her "cooped up," as her phrase had it, in her apartment at the northeast corner of the village. She relied on frequent quick excursions as a way of seeing people and mingling with the world. But the winter had made even local trips of a few blocks—to church, to the post office, to the grocery—treacherous, and it made longer ones to nearby neighboring towns—to the bank or the beauty parlor—unthinkable.

So on a January morning, ten days before, she'd stood at her kitchen window with a bad case of cabin fever and looked out to see what she *had* been seeing—a morning world of undulant white running to the horizon. But she also saw something she hadn't—a high and cloudless sky. At the same time, she was listening to a radio forecast that promised another numbingly cold day, but one with no new snow, and she decided on impulse to get into her car and drive the four blocks to the market, not because she needed food, the grocer made deliveries, but because she needed another nourishment: to get out of her apartment for even half an hour and never mind the temperature.

I picture her getting into her boat-sized Buick and driving the empty, snow-surfaced small town streets at the crawling speed of vigilance. For most of her life she'd had a well-deserved reputation as a lead-foot at the wheel. Growing up, I overheard amused, exaggerated accounts of her daredevil driving—of our blue Dodge zipping through the village or passing someone on the highway as though his car were standing still. She liked to drive and she liked cars. She paid attention when the new models were introduced each year and, as with every other thing under the sun, she held strong opinions about them: which ones were attractive and which were not. She'd absolutely coveted a Ford Thunderbird in its original missile-sleek incarnation.

She reached the store and climbed out of the Buick. The tip of her cane on snow and ice was surely unable to sound the neat, even clicking that it made on the linoleum and thin carpet in her apartment. She negotiated the low curb, stepped up onto the sidewalk, and in falling did no damage either to her new hip or to the one God gave her. Instead, this time, she cracked her pelvis and broke her wrist.

As he'd sat in his car in the frozen dawn waiting to phone me, my brother had been thinking about the similarity of this morning and, except for the weather, the one last summer after her first fall. Then, as now, he'd been waked around four o'clock as he slept on her couch to hear a nurse say she'd had quite a bad night. Then, as now, he'd become alert in a moment. And in the brief time it took him to dress and gulp down his morning Coca-Cola and hurry to the hospital, she had rallied against every expectation. Entering her room, his arrival startled her. In her struggle through the night she'd been somewhere, in some private and primal version of life, and residually that's still where she was. And she had startled him almost as much because of how she looked—her color an unearthly white and her eyes darkly circled; a haggard and spectral kabuki face. Later, a nurse told him that when he was telephoned our mother had had effectively no blood pressure. The nurse said she'd never witnessed someone so close to death returning so quickly and so fully.

How would she be *this* time? This is what my brother wondered as he'd sat, waiting to call me, and watched the sun begin to light the winter day. How many times can a life elude aggressive failure?

The short, round nurse in charge of getting me ready looked down to consult her clipboard. "So I see it's the left eye we're doing this morning?"

I confirmed it was and she stuck a piece of tape to my forehead over my left eye. This seemed a protocol of spectacularly low-tech efficiency, which both did and did not reassure me.

My mother would be eighty-seven years old in May, when Iowa would be thawed and once more greenly habitable. She'd lived all but three of those years within a fifteen-mile radius of her present apartment, half of a low, blond-brick bungalow, where she moved six months after my father died. All her siblings had died as well. She was maybe two inches more than five feet tall at her full adult height, and she'd shrunk quite a lot over the last decade or so. Among the things she'd survived in her life, in chronological order as I remember them, were these: the removal of her thyroid gland; an operation that required one of her ribs to be taken out so that surgeons could get to the spot on her lung an X-ray had found, a spot that proved to be nothing of concern; quadruple bypass surgery; cancer of the cheek, whose aggressive excavation made it necessary to pull every tooth in her mouth; a mild stroke that caused a gap of several hours when she couldn't remember anything of the belligerent nonsense she spoke to the two or three people, including a favorite niece, who happened to phone her in that time and who'd been naturally alarmed—*So unlike your mother*—and inevitably a little offended—*Still, no one appreciates being talked to like that*; two heart attacks within a few days of each other, the second while she lay in the hospital recovering from the first; two bouts of severe pneumonia that put her in the hospital for weeks and left her with a chronic phlegmy cough; and, this past August, the broken hip and the resulting surgical replacement and rehabilitation.

I don't remember her having cataract surgery, but the odds make it extremely likely that she did. Maybe I have no memory of it because it would have seemed the equivalent of her catching a cold in the context of the serious assaults on her body. None of which, nor their accumulation, made her for a moment an invalid. She'd vowed to return the aluminum walker she used while getting accustomed to her new hip, and she had met that goal, graduating to just a cane, the rhythmic click I've described of its tip on her floors like the quick, even ticking of her life's second hand.

I tended to say she was simply too *mean* to let her body give in to a more than temporary setback, intending it to be an admiring acknowledgment of her flinty resolve. But I'd learned to be careful where I said it, thanks to a conversation months ago, after her first fall, with the manager at her bank who asked me how she was doing. She was beloved by everyone at the bank, and when I gave my customary answer to the manager's question she shot me a look of startled disapproval.

ॐ

"What's your history?" the short, round nurse asked me.

"What's my history?"

"Any previous surgeries?" she asked.

Ah. *That* history. I mentioned a major operation on my left knee to remove a badly torn medial meniscus when I was twenty-one, in those prehistoric days before arthroscopic surgery. I've always liked saying "medial meniscus." It's one of the few terms I know that suggests I have any knowledge of the anatomy. I'm familiar with the knee's anterior cruciate ligament and the shoulder's rotator cuff and the plantar tendon that runs taut like the string of a bow along the sole of the foot. I know these body parts because they're the ones that athletes commonly injure and my interest in sports is an addiction, deep and long. But in general I've been oddly incurious over the course of my life about the way the body works and what holds it together, or doesn't. I suppose this is a symptom of an attitude about my own, the arrogant fantasy that it was uniquely impervious to age.

"Never had your tonsils out?" asked the short, round nurse.

"Oh, right. Yes. When I was really young."

She finished with her forms, then steered me in my upright bed across the room and parked me again. Next she asked me to tilt my head back while she put dilating drops in my eye. When she'd finished, a large, doughy-bodied anesthesiologist wearing surgical scrubs and a plastic shower cap, his black-rimmed glasses pushed up on his forehead, walked with a bear-like shuffle toward me. He asked my name to make sure I was the person, with the history, the overhead monitor said I was. Then, with a minimal shake of his head, he said, "I'm sorry, but you can't be sixty-two." And in that moment was the ignoble essence of where I often found myself at this point in my life—all my vanity in play and hopelessly matched against the contradictions of time and evidence. There I was, a man on a collapsible gurney in a surgical clinic come to have the first of two cataracts removed, and I seized, with the need of an aging coquette, the words of someone telling me I looked younger than I was. Because I used to hear such words, that announced disbelief, routinely, and they verified for me—far more than I'd like to admit—the shallow sense of how I saw myself: nimble and ageless; my body, as I said, insusceptible.

Sad to say, I've continued to wait an expectant beat for that voice of surprise. But for some while now I've heard it only rarely, and whenever I don't my mind stumbles forward through the silent space of the exchange that doesn't happen, like someone pushing against the anticipated resistance of a door that opens freely. But here was this sweetly ursine shower-capped anesthesiologist who'd just said what he'd said, and the size of my gratitude was really pathetic.

He adjusted his black-framed glasses on his nose and took my hand, scanning the back of it for a plump and easy vein. He chose one he liked, his way with a needle was impeccable, and the flow of sedation began. Next he injected lidocaine into a corner of my eyelid to keep my eye still and me from feeling pain. Then he went away and when he returned a few minutes later, he had with him his oxygen on wheels. He gently clamped the plastic tubing to my nostrils. His face looked even fleshier than it had, the bags beneath his eyes grown fat as tiny purses. Which is to say, the sedative was already working; a luxurious lulling was moving in me.

But I was still alert enough—or more likely I was sufficiently sedated—to receive the unbidden coincidence that suddenly arrived. I sensed all at once my mother's presence; I felt it almost palpably; here were the two of us at exactly this moment, in Iowa and in Boston in our hospital beds, attached to our IVs, with slender plastic tubes sending oxygen up our noses. I was not in any way comparing the urgency of our hours, the brief inconvenience of my morning against the horrible struggle she was going through in hers. Simply, it struck me that, right then, we must look the same, with our networks of tubes and their air and their fluids, and I felt glad to have this moving illusion of her company, and with it the idea that she had mine; to be seeing her and me, a split-screen picture, in my mind. It was as if, with my thoughts and senses set free to roam, this was how they'd contrived to reach her.

Then came two familiar, floating moments that I've always thought of as my first memories. In one, I'm a small child lying in the dark in a hospital bed with a crib's slatted sides. I hear the sounds of other small children around me—the rustling of sheets, their soft fussing and steady breathing. I'm very frightened, feeling piercingly alone, and when I call my mother's name she answers from where she sits, somewhere near but not visible, off to the side and slightly behind me in the darkness.

In the second moment I am again that infant, now in her arms, leaving the hospital on a cold winter morning, like this one in Boston and hers in Iowa, and the vivid sensual instant is of her tucking me more securely into the warmth of her wool coat while covering my head with a blanket against a lightly falling snow. It's an even quicker flash than the first, little more than a sensory blink, and as close to womb-return as I can fathom.

Whether these are memories of the time when I was barely three and having my tonsils removed, or whether they're fragments of dreams that have taken up ethereal residence in the same way memories do, this I can't know.

I *do* know it's inexcusably mawkish to write—in the tone I've just sounded, with the details I've chosen—that these memories or dream-images or whatever they are arrived in concert with the thought that my mother and I were similarly hooked up. But that's what happened. Blame the nurse. She's the one who asked about my tonsils.

With the patch taped over my eye, I made my way down the three stone steps to our condominium door, unlocked it, and hung my coat in the tiny foyer. On the ride home I'd been a fairly dazed passenger alongside my friend, Sam, who'd generously insisted on picking me up.

Inside, I walked down the hallway to the phone and called my brother, leaving a message that assured him at rambling length that my head was clear enough to talk, though I had the sensation as I spoke these words that I had no role in forming them.

Half an hour later, when I got up from bed to answer his return call, he immediately began to tease me, saying I'd sounded in my message like a drunk trying to convince a cop he's sober. Thinking now about his chiding, I'm reminded of a Boston friend, another émigré from the middle of the country, saying that you know a Midwesterner is about to deliver bad news when you're surprised by his phone call and the first thing he does is ask about your weather. And that the news is really bad if the second thing he does is to tell you about his.

My brother was not exactly asking about my weather. I think of him, instead, as wishing to establish an instant intimacy, for we've learned over the years that the private joking insult is our lingua franca, through which we find a quick, fraternal ease.

"How's she doing?" I asked.

"No," he said, all mischief gone from his voice. "No, she didn't make it."

His words took me to a summer night in 2001. I was saying good-night to four friends who'd come to dinner to help me celebrate my birthday when the phone rang and I picked it up to hear my mother say, "Well, Dad didn't make it." She'd gotten right to it. She was too tired and too empty and, despite what seemed the eager purpose with which my father had been failing, too stunned to care about the weather; not mine; not hers; not then.

My brother was phoning from the road. He'd called her neighbor and close friend, Sue, and her sister-in-law, our Aunt Beverly, Aunt B. He'd talked to the funeral director and made preliminary plans for a service and now he was headed home.

Hours earlier, from the parking lot, after saying goodbye and wishing me luck, he'd gotten out of his car, still the only one in the visitors' lot, and made the short icy walk to the entrance. Inside, he took the back stairway to the second floor and started down the hallway, a dark tunnel at this hour with the wall lights dimmed and the patients asleep behind closed doors. The silence and the hour and the darkness made him feel a kind of weirdly privileged access, one he'd have been more than happy not to claim. The floor's only lighted room, at the hallway's end, was our mother's, and as he walked toward it he could see a nurse framed in the doorway. When he got close enough so that the sound of his footsteps reached her, she looked up, then turned to tell a second nurse that he'd arrived.

He walked in and before he could take in the room and our mother in her bed, the first nurse stepped forward like a too-eager hostess. She said, "Your mom is taking her last breaths." Her Midwestern twang was delicate with kindness. She moved aside then and he saw her.

She was sitting straight up in her raised bed, her posture a supplicant's. Her eyes were wide and looking through her glasses at nothing—and what, that could possibly matter, was there to see? He watched her lunge forward for air, her toothless mouth stretched wide—a beak, as the image came to him; a baby bird's for food.

My brother walked over and sat down next to her. She was oblivious to his presence, to the nurses, to the external world, so fiercely was she inside her need to breathe. He saw that any words from him were quite beside the point; he could only watch her gasps, which were cadent and all-effortful as she leaned forward and then fell back against her pillow, a small ferocity in this rhythm of trying not to die. She had the strength to make the effort a few more times, three, four, her dying keeping time, until the cadence asked her to make another, and she didn't.

The nurse who'd greeted my brother approached her and put

a stethoscope to her chest while she held her wrist. After a moment she looked at him and said, "She's passed."

He nodded.

The nurse told him to stay as long, to take as much time, as he wished. Then she and the other nurse turned to leave, carefully shutting the door behind them.

Now the quiet was a presence, that presence which only the moment after death can fashion, a quiet we experience as having heard, as knowing well, the first time we hear it. Through his numbness he wondered what his grief should do. Should he be crying? If so, why wasn't he, since the lump in his throat that kept him from tears was much smaller than his sadness? Should he say something to her, as he'd known not to do moments before when she was distractedly alive?

Moments before when she was alive. The phrase, or something like it, resonated, and with it he felt death's frankness, felt the absence of all subtlety. And just after that he felt precisely the opposite: he sensed how uncapturably nuanced death was. These were feelings, purely—far from anything he thought. What he *thought* was that she didn't look to be at peace—the mourner's requisite assessment of a body in a casket. *She's at peace now. She looks so peaceful.* To him, she didn't look peaceful at all; she looked actively spent, worn out to a depth of exhaustion more valid than death.

He thought about his visits to her here, sitting in this chair next to her bed, fighting the wish to leave when there was nothing more to say and nothing else to feel. Now, when she couldn't take a pulse of comfort from his staying, he felt not urgency but inexperience at the thought of leaving her. What rules, what etiquette were there that could help him? How brief was too brief, how long too long?

As he studied her face, it seemed to him strange in the extreme that she was still wearing her glasses. Whatever you believed about where she was now, about matters of the soul, where hers was, *if* it was, surely she'd be managing perfectly without her glasses. He reached over and took them off and put them in his coat pocket.

And then at some point he found that he was standing, with no memory that he'd stood. He looked down at her once more and noted, as he had when he arrived, that there were no feeding tubes, no monitors, no oxygen supply. She'd had only her unassisted breath to help her gather and collapse, gather and collapse, as she made her last great appeal to her body's meanness.

So I had been mistaken. We had not been joined, my mother and I. We'd not been twinned in the moment, half a continent apart, by our IVs and our breathing tubes as we lay in our raised beds. We'd not been allied except as a contrivance, through the unseemly ease of my imagination. I would need to think on our history, hard and patiently, before it could be more than heavy-handed metaphor to say that I'd begun to see the world clearly on the day, in the hour, my mother died.

TENACITY

WE STOOD, SURROUNDING THE GRAY MARBLE GRAVESTONE.
It was one of hundreds rising up out of the snow in long, straight rows like a bumper winter crop. There'd been no new storms for several days, the winter now refined to a wind that raked your face.

This cemetery was a spot of intimately familiar earth, where my brother, Bob, and I had buried our father almost seven years before and where we'd come as children for our grandparents' funerals. This morning, there were Sue and I, my brother and his wife and their three grown sons, along with the funeral director and the Methodist pastor, a thin, smooth-skinned, soft-voiced man named Reverend Riggle.

He was speaking of the certainty of my mother's eternal reward, which she'd earned at least in part by her devoted service to the church. In the five days since her death, I'd been thinking off and on about the nature of her faith. By which I mostly meant that I'd been trying to imagine how *she* had imagined the stuff, the substance of an afterlife; that substance of the things she might have hoped for, that evidence of the things she'd not seen, as the letter to the Hebrews speaks of faith.

As I listened to Reverend Riggle's version of the contract with eternity, I felt an easy scorn, quick as an adolescent's for anything adult, and I wanted to be more generous than that. I was here, after all, on my dead mother's, on the reverend's, on the culture's terms, and I should honor them. Particularly since there had been a time when I did, when I was a boy and an ardent, humorless believer.

Sitting in church with my parents on Sunday morning, I repeatedly looked past the minister at the pulpit to the backdrop of a maroon velvet drape that hung from the ceiling to the floor covering the wall behind the altar. At some point I had come to understand that behind this drape was a secret, luxuriously furnished room and back there, in that room, was where God was. I knew of course that His primary residence was Heaven, so I didn't presume He lived in the room behind the drape in any daily way. I thought of it as a kind of *pied à terre*, a place He escaped to now and then, a relaxing weekend in rural Iowa.

But here's the point: that God—the long, white beard, the long, white robe, the elegant wooden staff—that He was back there relaxing on His second-home throne was nothing I fantasized. It was the thrilling truth and I wouldn't have dared to sneak up in the quiet of an empty sanctuary to pull the drape aside and take a peek. Not that I feared the crushing disappointment of looking at a naked wall. It was, rather, a matter of delicious intimidation as I carried the sense of God's majesty, the wattage of His radiance, not to mention his Old Testament temper if you crossed Him.

So in thinking about my mother's long Methodist life, I'd been wondering whether at the end of it she'd embraced some adult version—whatever that meant—of my early boyhood's literal belief. Or had she come to an understanding, or maybe always held it, that led her to a more metaphorical faith? It was a conversation she and I had never had.

At the gravesite, the cold was posing us all like waifs, our bodies tightly clenched inside our heavy coats. Our eyes were watering; our noses were running. I looked past Reverend Riggle to the vast white landscape of fields fertile with winter and heard him pray, "We beseech thee, O Lord, to dispense your perfect kindness to those loved ones gathered here as we commend your servant, Maudie, to your loving care."

We all turned and started toward our cars to drive the short distance to the church. The sky was now a mist and the mist was crystalline, making the wind hurt even more. Still, I paused a moment at the stone sitting squatly in the snow, taken with the feeling, brief as a breath, that I was abandoning my mother, and my father, to this unspeakable weather, and the phrase came to the disrespectful adolescent in me: You could catch your death out here.

Ten days back in Boston, I left our condominium to take a fifteen-minute walk through my South End neighborhood and the edge of Chinatown to Tufts-New England hospital where I had an appointment for an echocardiogram.

My heart had been behaving somewhat oddly for a few months. It would, for no reason I could trace, all at once begin to beat with a particularly emphatic percussion. It didn't happen often, but often enough, and when I felt it pounding most intensely I imagined a claustrophobic microbe beating frantically, metrically, on the walls of my heart.

Recently, my cardiologist had seen me to review the results of a heart monitor I'd worn for nearly twenty-four hours, during which my heart beat 89,219 times. In his office, he'd asked me to sit down and leaned toward me with a pencil and a drawing pad.

His name is Andrew Weintraub. He is fair-complected, bespectacled, in his mid- to late forties I would guess, and his manner, which is brisk, is saved from being brusque because his hurrying intelligence is entirely friendly; it's a knowledgeable energy he's happy to dispense. Still, he gives the impression of being perennially en route and he quickly drew a kindergarten-simple sketch of the heart, getting its inverted-fat-acorn shape exactly right.

Then he divided it into its four chambers: two upstairs, the atria, two below, the ventricles.

Technically, my mother died of congestive heart failure, and it came to me as Dr. Weintraub drew and talked about the heart that he was inversely narrating the physiology of her death: the sequence of valves opening (as the orifice of hers inexorably narrowed) and blood flowing (as hers therefore couldn't) from top (where hers was forced to stay) to bottom (where it couldn't get).

The day I'd worn the monitor, only 190 of my 89,219 heartbeats were irregular. But few as they were, there were enough of them to identify the beat as something called supraventricular tachycardia. Dr. Weintraub had explained what this was by returning to his drawing and inking a tiny button in the left atria. It's called the sino-atrial node, and in a normally working heart it's from here that an electrical impulse is evenly, repeatedly sent out to start and keep the beat.

Sometimes, though, other heart cells, as though jealous, or bored, connive to intercept the node's essential task and prematurely fire away. These impulses, once released, have no idea where to go or what to do so they zip around in the heart, producing a kind of wild short-circuiting. No wonder in such moments my entire upper body felt caught in a riptide of pulse, felt as if it were actually swaying to the strength of these renegade charges.

Walking to my echocardiogram appointment on this bright, cold January morning, I passed a small group of homeless men gathered on a street corner. One of the South End's long-established features is a scattering of shelters, notably the city's largest, the Pine Street Inn—which is hardly the cozy auberge its name suggests, but an enormous painted-brick building that runs the length of a city block.

I worked for some years as a Pine Street volunteer. I stood at the receiving desk of the medical clinic for three hours, one night a week, and greeted the men and recorded their names as they stood in line for its various services. Several needed to take their medications, which the nursing staff kept for them. But many came for things I could dispense myself. Some stopped to receive a nightly packet of Tylenol and vitamins. Several came in and dropped, dead-weighted, into a chair while I drew plastic tubs of soapy water so they could soak their feet, which were leprously scabbed and stank unimaginably and as often as not were missing toes. Most of these men were drunk or high and hacking convulsively. Some, schizophrenic, were speaking to their voices, debating apparently contrasting accounts of what had happened to the pair of them that day. One night a man, his feet resting in their warm bath, his pants legs rolled up past his calves, broke off his private conversation, turned to me, and calmly began: "My name is Yves Saint Pierre. In Chicago, I am known as Jesus Christ. My inner fire is so strong, I can be with a woman who has VD and I won't get VD." He continued, still serenely instructive: "Everything is color and energy. White is the brightest on the side of negative energy. Forty thousand cosmic vibrations. Red is the highest positive energy. Eighty-five thousand cosmic vibrations."

Over the years at Pine Street, I watched men get thinner and thinner. I noticed more and more of their teeth falling out. I saw faces altered by knife gashes and mashed-in noses. I observed their limps growing increasingly severe, until they needed canes, and after canes, crutches, and after crutches, wheelchairs. They lived, these men, dog years of illness and abuse: one year aged them seven.

As I passed the cluster of men this morning, I recognized quite a few of them, though none gave me a second look. I began to recall them individually—Bobby, whose entirely toothless mouth caused his face to collapse in on itself like a worn-out shoe; Teddy, dark featured, swarthy, imperviously handsome, his eye patch giving him the look of a silent-movie star playing a swashbuckling buccaneer; Eric, a cheerful man who always called me The Riddler, insisting I was a dead ringer for that Jack Nicholson character in the Batman movies. There were a couple of others whose names I'd forgotten, but my thought about them as a group was, My god, how can you, and you, and you, still be alive? There I was, headed off to the hospital, my heart—as it happened right then—banging away in my chest. And there they were, their faces weather-burnished, their camaraderie high-spirited, having spent the night on narrow cots in a crowded shelter dormitory, sleeping away the booze and the drugs of the previous day, and now well into their frigid Boston mornings.

In the echocardiogram room I lay shirtless on my side while a technician, seated next to me, held the instrument's sensor, which looked vaguely like a stethoscope's medallion and was connected by a long cord to a console fitted with several dials and a fairly small screen. She'd applied some kind of jelly to the sensor to aid the transmission of images, and now she began to guide the sensor incredibly slowly over my heart.

This was at the same time an oddly intimate and deeply alien sensation—stripped to the waist, with this stranger of a woman tracing, more deliberately than you could imagine, some jelly-slathered device all around my chest, while both of us watched the grainy moving images of my heart on the little screen; it was like impossibly cautious sci-fi foreplay.

I found the images enthralling, not least for the accompanying machine-amplified sound effects—the regular sloshing and flushing of my blood as it flowed up and down and in and out of my heart's four chambers. I pictured someone in thigh-high waders moving through floodwaters.

"What a cool machine," I said to the technician.

And she replied, "Jack Nicholson."

"What?"

"It's named 'Jack Nicholson.'"

". . . Why?" I asked.

"We give them all a name," she said, the sum and substance of her explanation.

What filled Jack Nicholson's screen was gorgeously patterned, and grayly abstract unless you knew what you were seeing. It looked, with its lighter flecks among the gray and its smoky swirls, like the Milky Way. Or maybe it looked, with its beckoning cavities, like a series of caves, a spelunking world. Except that everything was moving, endlessly, regularly moving; valves opening and closing like saucy tongues lewdly flicking; dark holes pulsing primordially. So maybe it looked like a fetus with attitude from the Pleistocene Age, although if I were a Pleistocene mother, the fetus I was watching was not depending on me for its life; I was dependent on it for mine.

Viewing an echocardiogram, compared to looking at an X-ray, is like reality television compared to still photography, and I realized that part of the pull for me was voyeuristic. Even as this professionally decorous technician with her gooey probe was Geiger-countering her way all over my chest, I felt, for my part, a kind of Peeping Tom, for what I was watching on the screen seemed to be behaving entirely on its own. The flow and gurgle and animation were completely independent of anything I was asking my body to do or was otherwise aware that it was doing, and it seemed as if I were catching these moving parts of me unawares.

As I lay there, a sense of great gratitude came over me. There was my heart, working away on my behalf without notice or complaint as it had with no pause for more than sixty years—a self-assigned responsibility; an act of pure charity. Watching, it seemed a marvel that its recent small mistakes were its first.

I felt particularly close to it, too, because I see it working practically. Or mechanically. It is of course a pump, life's splendid pump; and there is magic to be sure in the idea of the electrical charge that gets it started and keeps it going. Still, given its elementary design and the sequential way it works, it suggests a device that someone like my father, someone tremendously clever at fashioning gadgets to solve a particular barnyard need, might build from spare parts he had lying around in his shop out in the garage. The heart seems to me just such a sublime *contraption* and in that spirit I imagined my mother's, wheezing, sputtering, held together with caulking and patches of crisscrossed duct tape, until finally exhausted.

When the technician finished, she said, "You gave us some good pictures." She pronounced it "pitchers." I heard this as her applauding my heart's commendable behavior, a quality of performance I might take some credit for. I ate healthily. I exercised vigorously. It only followed that my heart would be photogenic. Ready for her compliment, I asked, "What makes some people's pictures better than others?" She shrugged. "Some days they're good, some days they're not. Nobody knows."

A few hours later, I saw Dr. Weintraub and he prescribed what he termed "a homeopathic dosage" of a beta blocker, a class of drugs which, simplistically put, quiets those renegade short-circuit-causing cells. He also asked me to wear another monitor, and to wear it not for a day but for a month.

Compared to the first one, it was the size of an iPhone instead of an old VHS cassette, and more sophisticated in what it recorded, which meant more complicated to operate. If I felt my heart beating strongly, however slightly more than normal, I was to push a button to start the monitor recording. After that, I was to call an 800 number, where, like infomercial operators, technicians were standing by. Then I had to put the monitor up to the receiver to send what I'd caught on tape to their transcribing equipment. In other words, I would, for a month, be bugging my heart.

It was a Sunday afternoon when I got back to Iowa and my mother's apartment. The temperature was as stunningly cold as it had been three weeks before when we'd stood at the gravesite and a wind of ice had pricked our faces. As I'd driven from Boston across the northern plains there'd been a storm a day in front of me and one a day behind, and for the length of the trip I stayed inside a frozen calm these parentheses of weather made.

With me on the drive were two of our three dogs—a cairn terrier and a curly-haired French basset whose breed name is so long it goes by its initials, PBGV. They'd been peerless pals and exemplary travelers. They'd slept for hours in the rear of the hatchback, never asking if we were there yet, predictably delighted with my choice of rest stops, and beyond delighted, thrilled, with whatever motel would have us at the end of the day, sniffing the perimeter of the room like ATF hounds and checking under the bed for vending-machine crumbs the maids' vacuum cleaners might have missed.

Almost everything my mother owned was being donated to the church, to be sold or dispersed however Reverend Riggle and the congregation decided. Volunteers would be coming later in the week to sort and tag and organize it all, which left me literally free of any heavy lifting. I was there to clean out drawers and closets, mark some things my brother wanted, fill enormous trash bags, and box her books to take to the town library.

The fall on the ice that broke her wrist and more critically her pelvis left her immobilized. Unable to get out of bed and begin to take some aided infant-timid steps, her body could not call on her heart to exert itself. With perilously little to do, its already weak valves, as I said, began to close, so that its blood could barely flow, until the strength it needed to keep that blood moving was more strength than it had.

It was the second fall she'd taken. The first, four months earlier, occurred as she stood at her kitchen counter fixing supper. At shortly after six o'clock on a warm late-summer evening she'd finished slicing a tomato, turned away from the counter, and in turning lost her balance and fell to the hard linoleum floor. She momentarily blacked out and when she regained consciousness she rightly suspected, through her pain, that she'd broken her hip. She knew she couldn't get up, and the apartment's only telephone sat on an end table just inside the doorway in the adjoining TV room.

In the hours that followed, she crawled toward the phone, stopping several times to rest, several more times briefly passing out, and calling for help as loudly as she could over the sound of the television. Its volume, as my brother once affectionately joked, was typically raised to such a decibel that if you sat in front of it the g-force of the sound smushed your face like a pilot's at warp speed. She called first when she heard her young neighbor through their duplex's common wall, returning home with her boyfriend. She called to them over and over, but all they heard was the television going late into the night, which did arouse the young woman's curiosity, until her boyfriend reminded her the old lady often fell asleep in front of her blaring TV set.

She also called when her thoughtful neighbor in the house next to the duplex stepped into the tiny vestibule to drop her mail, which he'd picked up at the post office earlier that day. And she called at dawn when the deliveryman left the Sunday newspaper at her door.

This pattern of pain, and pausing to rest, and calling out in vain continued until, at six in the morning, twelve hours after she'd fallen, she got her body to the doorway that led into the TV room, and was able to crawl partially through, and reached for the phone and dialed 911.

Now I was standing at her sink, where she had stood that summer evening before she turned and lost her balance. I turned and, placing heel to toe, walked off the distance of her crawl. It was fifteen steps, roughly five yards; she'd progressed slightly more than a foot per hour.

I wanted to imagine the cruel calisthenics of her ordeal. I walked back to the sink and got down on the floor, my body just fitting between the kitchen table in the center of the room and the bright-blue wooden cabinets that ran the length of a wall. She must have rolled over and lain on her right side to keep her weight from pressing on the pain of her left hip, which meant that for twelve hours, except when she lost consciousness, she was looking at these bright-blue cabinet doors two inches from her nose. I crawled along on my right side, wondering how she had crawled, from where in her tiny old body the strength had come. Had she pushed with her right leg, pulled with her right arm, a kind of sidestroke? Had she alternately tucked and extended her body like an inchworm on its side, which would have surely been excruciating? I stopped crawling, trying to picture how she'd arranged herself when she had stopped, whether she'd laid her head on her cushioning right arm or simply rested it on the linoleum. I assumed she'd stayed strictly on her right side even when she called for help, in which case she was lying turned away from her apartment's front door, making her thoughtful neighbor dropping her mail and the person delivering her Sunday newspaper even less able to hear her.

I got to the doorway and crawled through into the TV room, lying now on the thick, mustard-colored carpet. I looked up to the end table where the phone sat. She would have reached with her left arm and knocked the phone to the carpet, then pressed the big senior-sized buttons: 9, 1, 1.

When the local ambulance arrived, the driver noted that she was terribly hoarse; she'd virtually lost her voice from calling out repeatedly.

That night, I lay awake on her couch, the dogs curled up on the floor next to me, her living room to them just another wisely chosen motel at the end of the day. Whenever I'd visited her she always insisted I take the bedroom—claiming she often slept on the couch anyway. But the idea of doing that on this trip, of sleeping in her bedroom, was unthinkable and the very strength of that unfathomability made it clear—not that I needed the clarity—how sharply I was feeling the presence of her absence. And maybe, in fact, the dogs felt it too—at least Willie, the terrier, who'd walked into the empty apartment on our arrival and to my astonishment immediately lifted his leg against her favorite chair, as if to leave his mark on a thing that had been dearly hers.

I lay on her couch thinking about people falling down and unable to get up. For a few years I rented an office space in a converted warehouse near the Pine Street shelter. One morning I happened to look down from my third-floor window and spotted a group of maybe half a dozen habitual guests drinking with ambition at ten A.M. They were standing on the steps of an opposite warehouse entryway, arranged in tiers, like some debauched choral group. As I was about to turn away from the window, one of the men on the top step suddenly lost his balance and fell into the chest of a companion on the step below, causing this man to fall into a third and the third into a fourth until all but one of them—he, on crutches, was somehow still standing—lay on their backs on the snowy sidewalk. A few of them began to struggle to get up, though they were clearly too drunk to do so, their arms flailing at their sides, as if feebly attempting to make angels in the snow, while their comrade crutch-cantered back to the shelter for help. Shortly, an ambulance arrived and two EMTs emerged to tend to the fallen.

I was working at the clinic by coincidence that night and I happened to spot the man—his name was Richard—who'd gone for help as he was standing in line, leaning on his crutches, waiting to get supper. He said, when I asked him, that his day had been good, fine, nothing special, just hanging with his buddies and trying to stay warm. His face had that look of ruddy emaciation I'd come to think of as particular to the homeless who spend their days outdoors steadily losing their health while the bodies they live in fight with a separate tenacity to keep it.

My final errand on my way out of town was to return the Lifeline signaling machine to the hospital. My brother and I had tried to persuade her to get the service a few years before, after her two heart attacks. She'd explained her reluctance by saying that, for her, one of the hardest parts of being old was asking someone to lend her a hand, for anything. That she couldn't help but think of even the easiest request as an imposition. And though she knew it was silly, she saw pushing the Lifeline button as finally that, an imposition.

I didn't doubt she felt this; it was entirely consistent with who she was and how she thought. But I also believe and believed at the time the greater reason she resisted was her sense that the button formalized and publicized her body's vulnerability.

Those twelve hours on the kitchen floor after her first fall were the argument we'd needed. If she'd been wearing the button she could have pushed it where she lay and help would have reached her in a matter of minutes.

Her second fall, the day she slipped on the ice in front of the grocer's, she was helped to her feet by someone passing by, likely someone she knew, and insisted she was fine. She'd somehow managed to drive the few blocks home, get out of the car and into her apartment, and she was sitting on her couch, watching her broken wrist swell and feeling her broken pelvis throb and asking herself whether or not to push the Lifeline button, when by sheer coincidence my brother called just to ask how she was doing.

"God, yes!" he said when she asked him if she should. So she did, she pushed the button for the first and only time.

As for the Lifeline machine, the thing itself, it wouldn't die. It sat on the end table next to her phone, and when I was ready to leave I pulled what seemed to be all of its several plugs. Some were connected to the phone, others to outlets in the wall, but it continued maddeningly to blink and to tell me that its battery was low, if I'd be so kind to check it. There was, I thought, a Midwest tenor in the voice: monotonic, slightly abashed, perhaps a bit hesitant to make its request but, unlike my mother, making it anyway. Finally, I got down on my knees and crawled behind the couch and found the wire I'd missed and yanked it from an outlet and at last the machine went dark and silent. I rose and wrapped its wires around it, dropped it in a paper bag, and opened the door to free the dogs into the bright Arctic day.

The car was packed. The dogs were ready. My heart monitor was holstered on my hip, its adhesive conducting pads attached as directed in three places on my chest; my homeopathic-strength beta blockers were secured in my Dopp kit.

Key in hand, I locked her apartment door. In doing so I sensed that I had no further claim, could leave no mark, on anything that was tangibly, physically hers. My heart began a quickened rhythm, a wild short-circuitry of regret and finished time, the cause of its beat for once explicable. For a moment the world was color and energy, cosmic vibrations, negative white and positive red, glorious evidence of things not seen.

I would reach the hospital in less than twenty minutes. There, I would return the Lifeline machine to the friendly main-entrance receptionist. I would watch her open her logbook and draw a line through my mother's name. It would have been absurd to expect anything other than the quick and cordial bit of business we would conduct, but nevertheless I would be struck that our exchange had all the solemnity of returning a cable box, when for me, in that moment, handing over the machine that had struggled not to die, would have the force of surrendering a soul.

In the two weeks I'd been wearing the monitor, I'd twice debated pushing the button. And twice I'd persuaded myself that if I wasn't sure whether or not my heart was beating oddly, well, then, obviously it was not.

WHAT WAS SERVED

༄

OUR FARMHOUSE SAT ATOP A SLIGHT RISE IN THE MIDDLE
of the acreage. The land, as lawn, sloped away from the foundation and flattened out in all directions until it met the surrounding
fields, then continued extremely as rows of corn and soybeans. A
wide, pillared porch wrapped around the north and east sides of
the house. As a boy, in summer, I sometimes paused in my play
to sit for a time on the porch railing and look into the eastern
distance. If my father and grandfather Bauer happened to be out
there, working in the field that was my view, I watched the two
of them on their tractors moving the day's tending implements
back and forth on the horizon.

And if the hour were any time from mid-morning till noon,
I could also turn, from that same perch on the porch, to look
through the screen door just a few steps away into our kitchen
where another kind of work was going on. There my mother
was preparing the full, hot midday meal, moving about the big
floral-patterned wallpapered room, frequently glancing out the
windows above the kitchen counter whose view was of that same
east field. A large fan sat on the floor in the doorway that opened
onto the small back porch. Its air moved futilely against the stove's

strong heat. A clock was mounted on the wall above the refrigerator, but she told the time by where the men were in the field.

Thinking back, I see my father and grandfather, their tractors and machines inching along at an almost imperceptible pace, their sounds made soundless by their distance from the house, while my mother in the kitchen was all bustle and noise. The sharp metallic clang of a spoon against a pot, stovetop burners rattling, oven door opening and thudding shut. And woven through it all, the voices from the radio that sat atop the refrigerator. The absentminded mumbles of Arthur Godfrey. Or "the real-life drama of Helen Trent, who . . . fights bravely, successfully, to prove what so many women long to prove, that because a woman is thirty-five or more, romance in life need not be over."

Remembering the agrarian stateliness of the tractors silently progressing, and the banging, short-order-cook urgency audible through the screen, what lingers is my impression that, compared to my father's and grandfather's work, my mother's was the harder and more manual labor.

My mother's father, my Grandpa Evans, began his life as a coal miner in the final years of the nineteenth century. A nomad of the bituminous landscape, he traced the Midwest's longitudinal seams, living in various company towns before settling with his new wife in the village of Colfax, in the center of Iowa.

He'd met and married the former Mary Jane Mabie in one of the mining hamlets where he'd worked. Over the next two decades they conceived ten children, six boys and four girls. My mother, born in 1921, was the third youngest. One of her sisters died in childbirth; another died from cancer in her early thirties. Her six brothers, as they grew to adolescence, became a pugnacious tribe, fiercely loyal to one another, a loyalty expressed within the rules of a shouting, scuffling fraternal etiquette: their version, you might say, of a rowdy mining camp.

My mother was known to some of her siblings and, later in

her life, to all of her nieces and nephews, as Tim, Aunt Tim. She embraced the nickname, for she hated her given name, Maude. And besides, the name was clearly bestowed with fondness, if with a fiendish edge, for Tim was the neighborhood cat that one of her brothers threw in her face when she was a girl, scratching her badly and making her terrified of cats all her life, chills running up and down her arms and legs and her cry of dismay, "Oh, god, there's a cat!," if she so much as caught sight of one. It's hard to imagine what trick of quick complexity her mind worked through every time she heard the name directed to her with affection.

All this gravely swarming life took place in a tiny two-story house that looked too tall for its foundation. The house leaned and sagged in important places—the porch roof, the cellar door— and was here and there leprous with peeling paint. Photos of my mother at various ages, from early childhood on, posing outside on a dirt-pocked patch of grass with one or some of her siblings, show the house as a backdrop, forever in a state of disrepair. There's the intimate gravity of Walker Evans images in these snapshots.

My grandfather Evans, then, presided over a crowded, raucous, impoverished domesticity that he did nothing to calm or financially ease. He came home from the mines each night, the grime on his hands and face like a minstrel's makeup. Standing naked outdoors whatever the weather, his clothes lying on the ground beside him like a pile of filthy pelts, in the privacy of twilight in a galvanized tub of water reaching almost to his knees, he roughly soaped his body clean, except for the cracks and crevices in his hands and fingers, permanent coal-black lines as fine as filament, after which he changed into a laundered shirt and overalls. Later, with supper finished, he remained at the oilcloth-covered kitchen table and drank himself into a quarrelsome humor, a brooding, often nasty figure his children learned early they should leave alone.

My mother graduated from high school in 1939. Along with

her degree, she earned a teaching certificate that licensed her for a position in the state's secondary schools. Among the hundreds of photographs she kept in books and envelopes, and in turn stored in boxes throughout her life, there is one of a vintage automobile, patches of snow on its top-hat roof and running boards, sitting in drifts up to its bumpers, across the street from the clearly recognizable Evans house. On the back of the photo she wrote at some point, "My first car, Model A." In its slumping modesty the Model A appears a kind of replica on wheels of the house across the street. She'd bought it to begin her working life at the age of nineteen as a country schoolteacher.

At first, she continued to live at home and drove back and forth to her school, seven miles away, a significant commute over country roads. After a year, she decided to board with a family whose farm was near the school. Her anxiousness at living on her own began to ease early on when, one Saturday at noon, sitting down with the family for sandwiches, she began to layer potato chips atop her luncheon meat before crunching them down with the top piece of bread. It suddenly occurred to her that this Evans routine might look strange at best, uncouth at worst, to someone outside the family. Alarmed, she glanced across the table to see the young wife and mother of the house doing precisely the same thing. At that moment she looked up from her plate, met my mother's eye, and the two of them exchanged sorority smiles.

My mother and father had known each other slightly in high school, but in a town and school so small everybody knows one another at least slightly. Besides, he was three years older, which at that age amounts to a generation's difference. His photo-studio graduation portrait shows a dashing young man in a three-piece suit, his tie smartly knotted (all his life he could execute a Windsor knot as perfect as the Duke's) and puffing stylishly above the V of his vest, a kind of peacock flaring. His pompadoured, Gallic-nosed handsomeness is saved from delicacy by the look in his eyes and the line of his lips that go beyond the hint that he has mischief in mind to a sly confidence that he can make that mischief happen.

In his first years after high school, he managed a gas station and garage but failed to make a go of it. He helped his father farm. He worked as a rural mail carrier. But that was his still undirected daylight life. Of his nights he was more certain. He was part of a small pack whose carousing escapades garnered them a reputation in the county's little towns. It was a life his mother's blindly indulgent parenting allowed him to pursue. (His one sibling was a sister, Beverly, ten years younger, so in a sense he was raised a pampered only child. As, a decade later, was she.) Another photo shows him flanked by two of his friends, the three of them leaning against a sleek sedan, its sheen and style in marked contrast to my mother's little Model A leaning vulnerably into snowdrifts. He is again dressed in suit and tie, his hands in the pockets of a long, dark wool topcoat, his fedora suavely tipped. He looks for all the world like a noir movie character: maybe the private detective with the society-family fortune, maybe the underworld boss in his custom-tailored clothes with his most trusted thugs flanking him.

I don't know the details of when my mother and father started dating, when as a couple they began to join his friends and their girlfriends for weekend nights in places like Pearl's—a country roadhouse a few miles north of town, just past a landmark the locals called The Curve, a severely sweeping bend of the two-lane highway to Des Moines—where they ate and drank and danced and laughed, nothing close to scandalous, nothing less than festive. Frequently, they drove to dances at the Val-Air Ballroom in West Des Moines, where all the best-known touring big bands played. Glen Miller. Tommy Dorsey. I picture them on the vast, dimly lit dance floor, my dapper father leading my pretty mother with a cautious grace, for he was a smooth, safe-stepping dancer.

From the Colfax *Tribune*, June 1942: "Miss Maude Evans, daughter of Mr. and Mrs. John E. Evans, and Mr. Kenneth Bauer, son of Mr. and Mrs. P. A. Bauer of Prairie City, were united in

marriage Friday evening, June 5, 1942, at the Methodist church. . . .
The bride is well and favorably known in the city, having grown
to womanhood here. She graduated from the Colfax high school
with the class of 1939 and since then has been a successful teacher
in the rural schools of the county.

"The groom also grew to manhood in this vicinity. . . . He is
a graduate of the Colfax high school with the class of 1936 and
since then, besides assisting in the management of his father's
farm, for a time operated the D-X Service Station in Colfax. . . .

"A reception for relatives of the bridal couple was held at the
Evans home immediately after the ceremony. . . .

"After a short honeymoon trip to the Black Hills, South Dakota,
they returned to Prairie City Tuesday to take up their residence
in an apartment at the home of his parents. He will assist in the
management of the Bauer farm, southeast of Prairie City."

The noontime meal my mother prepared for her husband and
her father-in-law every day but Sunday, from the first field work
in spring to the end of autumn harvest, was called *dinner*. Obviously, this made the only slightly less ambitious evening meal
supper. And what was typically for dinner? Maybe a roast of pork
with mashed potatoes and brown gravy. Maybe a baked ham with
her signature potato salad. (Its secret, she claimed, was substitut-
ing Miracle Whip for mayonnaise; go figure.) Maybe beef and
homemade egg noodles, or beef stew with carrots and potatoes
and onions, the noodles or stew beef simmering through the
morning in the pressure cooker, which gave a delicious meat-
sweet smelling humidity to the kitchen air.

I said that my mother's hours of preparation seemed ones of
mounting manual effort. Some days, I suspect, this was nothing
more than her rushing to have everything ready when the men
appeared. To make them wait to eat was to cost them precious
field time. But there was often something palpably more layered
going on in her as she moved about the kitchen, knowing that the

meal she was making would be followed not long after the dishes were done by the need to begin making another one—supper.

I don't mean to say she felt *uniquely* put upon. She was aware that her domestic chores were typical. In fact, she recognized that hers were fewer than those of many farmwives she knew who, in addition to all their household duties, shared much of the field work and livestock chores with their husbands. It's also true that my mother very much enjoyed her reputation as a cook, known among friends and family for her specialties. Oatmeal cookies, for one, crisp flat ovals that might better be called the Joy of Butter. And that potato salad for another.

Instead, I suspect that most everything that displeased and disappointed her about her life was distilled in that brooding humor. In any case, her sense of herself as a farm kitchen version of the *Woman in the Dunes* never left her, even decades after my father had sold the farmland and spent his time puttering and tinkering in his shop in the garage and, as often as not, came into the house around noon to make himself a sandwich. I remember her predictably complaining about her three young grandsons, my brother's sons, devouring those irresistible oatmeal cookies, which she'd baked expressly for their visit from St. Louis. Watching them return again and again to the big cookie jar on the kitchen counter, she shook her head after they'd left the room and, making her patented "Tsk!" sound with her tongue against her teeth, would say, not happily, to whoever she'd been talking to, "I just made these this morning and they're almost gone." What she saw in the nearly instantly empty jar was not the pleasure her food gave her grandsons, but rather the evidence that she must now make more of it.

On an early spring day in 1946, with a recently purchased used blue Chevrolet packed and ready, my mother and father and I, then seven months old, left a small apartment in a white clapboard house on Van Lennen Street in Cheyenne, Wyoming. My mother posed beside the car for a snapshot recording our departure. She wore a knee-length topcoat featuring a row of big round buttons running neck to hem. Her dark hat was a flat felt crown. She rested her hand on the Chevrolet's right front fender. Her smile had about it the nervous ambivalence of buyer's remorse.

We were headed back to Iowa. My father had been recently discharged from the Army, ending his splendidly unheroic military service as a sergeant in the dental corps at Fort Francis E. Warren on the scrub-grass outskirts of Cheyenne.

She had joined him there three years before. After they were engaged, assuming he would soon be drafted, they'd wanted to marry before his notice came and, not many months after they returned from their Black Hills honeymoon, it did. He reported to Fort Warren and began his duty, and as soon as she could, after the school semester ended, she organized her life and packed her belongings. Wanting to look her best for my father when she arrived, she bought a fashionable cream-colored light wool suit to wear on the long train trip, and at the age of twenty-two she left Jasper County, Iowa, for the first time. When she stepped from the train in Cheyenne, the accumulated engine soot and grime from the train had ruined her fashionable cream-colored suit; she greeted him looking as if she'd ridden all the way in the coal car with the tramps. It was a story she told on herself all her life.

In Cheyenne, for three years, their days unfolded in a kind, all-permissive present, a great, freeing distance from their past and from their future. Growing up, whenever I heard them speak of their years there, their voices became uniquely light and energetic. They remembered the Valencia Tavern, a downtown dive where my mother and her fellow clerks from the Montgomery Ward department store gathered after work. They remembered the endearing strangeness of their landlords' son, Carl, a sweet, simpleminded young man who spoke with a lisp and never learned to drive and rode his bicycle everywhere. Smiling, they remembered the nights my father smuggled bottles of pure alcohol out of the dental lab under the seat of his car to make bathtub gin for parties back at their apartment.

A large, glossy photograph from that time shows my mother with half a dozen other Montgomery Ward clerks posed outside the store, all of them wearing cowgirl hats and shiny western blouses. She and another young woman are crouching down in front, cigarettes in hand. They were all dressed for Frontier Days, a kind of annual cow-town Mardi Gras, much smaller, of course, and at least in their day striking a festive chord decibels quieter than New Orleans's lewd and lawless frolic. But it was plenty rambunctious nevertheless and a fine excuse to celebrate and sit on a curb and watch the parade and drink beer until you couldn't. Which was just what they, or at least my father, did.

So the lighthearted life they'd led before the war came to full flourish in their Cheyenne years. How could it not? There was everywhere a feeling in the air almost of obligation to live the war years fully. And surely my mother, taking pleasure in her husband's prankster energy, and taking some for herself and her version of it, was delighted she'd married a man who had it in abundance.

Once, looking at photos of my father in uniform, my mother in dresses and suits of the period, and in her Frontier Days cowgirl regalia, the notion briefly came to me that it was as if they were always in costume there. And I considered a kind of overarching metaphor—that they were dressing up for adult life in Cheyenne. And then I thought, no, more like the opposite: dressing up to postpone it, despite my infant presence.

Apart from the times I heard them recollect together, almost everything I know or infer about their history came from my mother. I don't remember talking with my father about the possible directions they imagined their life taking once the war was done. A few times, when she talked to me, she suggested he'd had thoughts of working with airplanes. Much of the activity at Fort Warren involved refitting aircraft for military use, and my father loved to visit the assembly hangars and—far more compelling than observing dental surgeries—watch the work and talk about it. It's a shame the Army hadn't assigned him that same duty; he was a gifted mechanic and he was fascinated by airplanes all his life (though his interest cooled as jet engines replaced propellers and, in his mind, the engineering of flight got too simple —not enough moving parts). All of this to say that he and my mother talked about possibly heading west after the war, to California and the burgeoning airplane industry.

Still, my mother insisted to me that she did not return to Iowa reluctantly. She said she'd missed the familiarity of life in the Midwest and that she missed her family, especially her mother and her two sisters, keenly. So she was pleased when her father-in-law, my Grandpa Bauer, wrote to tell my father that he wished to formally establish their farming partnership. He and my grandmother would be leaving the large, two-storied, many-gabled farmhouse to us and moving to the village of Prairie City, four miles northwest of the farm. For a short time, while we waited for them to organize their move, we would occupy the same small upstairs apartment my parents had lived in briefly before my father was drafted.

My mother knew my grandfather well enough to understand that his ambition was not to acquire more land, but rather for a kind of immaculate husbandry of the land he already owned, 140 acres, and 80 more he rented from an adjoining farm. It was enough, in 1946, to support two families, and it was ideally manageable for him and my father.

Whenever they remembered their time in Cheyenne, they'd recall the trip back to Iowa and the infinite flat-field boredom of the drive across Nebraska. It was an item in the history of their war years' episode, a piece of the lore.

"It seemed like a week to get across it."

"It's just the one state between Wyoming and Iowa, but it might as well be the whole country."

My father did not read books; my mother did, though I don't know if she ever read Cather's *My Ántonia*, with its narrator's recollection of arriving in Nebraska as a boy and seeing "nothing but land: not a country at all, but the material out of which countries are made. . . . I had the feeling that the world was left behind." My parents, of course, were simply passing *through* Nebraska, not arriving in it. But in any case, it was a trip, a tedium of seeing "nothing but land," they suffered only once. For all its extraordinary importance in their lives, they never revisited Cheyenne.

Doubtless, their minds and their moods on their departure had no reason to imagine they were leaving *the* world behind. They were merely leaving *that* world—yes, a golden one, but still—on their way to another that they were looking forward to. And I've decided they saw instinctively that their not returning preserved the size of the mythology and the vividness of the memories. Seeing it again, the war over, their friends gone, would have been for them like the experience of returning to the places of childhood and being startled at how small, how reduced, how ordinary everything is.

And maybe they knew, even as they were driving away from Cheyenne, that in the act of leaving it they were erasing it: that the moment they were gone, it was no longer there.

From my perch on the porch railing, a few minutes before or just past noon, I watched my father and grandfather bring their tractors to a stop, get down from their seats to unhook the plows or discs or whatever they were pulling, then climb back up and turn in the direction of the house. It was as if the kitchen's summoning smells had wafted out through the open windows into the thick summer heat and moved like an aromatic weather front until they reached my father and grandfather.

At that age—nine, ten, even eleven—I was beguiled by the world of early television westerns. (I once asked my fourth-grade teacher to call me by the surname Crockett, after Davy, on whom I was deeply fixated. She gave me, with her "No," an appropriately impatient frown.) Watching from our porch, I was a cavalry scout alert for any suspicious movement appearing suddenly out there on the rim of the world, and my father and grandfather were a pair of nasty Apaches on horseback pulling hijacked covered wagons.

When I saw them heading in, I called through the screen into the kitchen. "They're coming."

To which my mother replied, "Come help me set the table." And so, the real world returned. Cavalry scouts did not help set the table.

Inside, as we laid out the plates and cups and glasses, we soon heard the sound of the tractors, starting faint as rumors and growing as they got closer, until their loud, raw announcement of arrival in the barnyard, some fifty yards from the house. A minute, two minutes later, my father, in his blue chambray shirt and darker-blue loose-fitting jeans, and my grandfather in his shirt and pants of matching khaki, appeared on the back porch, removed their caps, and hung them on hooks. Their protected foreheads looked milk-white in contrast with the rest of their sun-browned faces. Farmer's tans.

Entering the kitchen, father and son and a life of shared tilling, they seemed intimately *teamed*. My father's face, compared to his high school graduation photo, had lost some of its lean angularity, softening his handsomeness without diminishing it. His thick, dark pompadour was matted down. The sweat band of his cap had made a line of dirt across his forehead. He greeted my mother and me and hurried into the small room next to the kitchen to wash up.

My grandfather chose a kitchen-table chair and sat down, waiting to go next. He remarked to my mother that whatever was for dinner smelled awfully good, which was both a compliment and the truth. He was a thin, hard-muscled man. His deep shyness gave him an air of courtliness. He walked with one hip permanently cocked from a boyhood accident, a broken leg and kneecap, that had left him unable to bend his leg. When he sat, that leg, his left, was extended stiffly like something that seemed to me, not artificial, but somehow independent of him. I saw it, and his resulting hitching gait, as the kind of exotic feature that distinguished heroes. Like a wound from a gunfight. Secretly, I sometimes practiced emulating it.

He was now a commuter, driving out to the farm every morning, the sun starting up the sky, from the little box of a house he and my grandmother had built in the village. I call it "little," but in fact it was as tiny as a cottage in a clearing in a fable, though, growing up, I didn't see it as particularly small. It sat on a large, corner lot—indeed, two adjoining lots—so there was plenty of space on which they could have built a bigger house. My grandfather, though not miserly, was always careful with his money, so perhaps that alone explains its size. Or perhaps, as much as he could, the farmer in my grandfather wanted to keep his double lot as open land and retain the sense of being surrounded by fields.

For me, those few miles from the farm to the village were the distance separating civilizations, as if the whole country, or at the very least Nebraska, lay between them. On overnight visits I brought my bicycle with me and rode it for hours, tracing and retracing the town's brief grid of streets. Sometimes my grandmother sent me on an errand to the grocery on the square. Pedaling furiously to the store and back again, I felt proprietary, purposeful, a thrillingly competent navigator of five blocks, which was to say, the world.

Sitting with my grandfather in their living room, I talked to him in detail about the baseball pennant races. I was a tedious pedant, steeped in scores and standings and statistics, and he listened patiently, feigning interest. For his part, he was an eager armchair geographer who loved to study maps and pore over atlases, and he took delight in quizzing me with questions. ("What's the capital of Alaska?" After a pause, my educated guess: "Juneau?" He, mishearing: "Mm-hum, *I* know. I'm asking, do *you*?")

Routinely we played checkers and routinely he trounced me, pointing out the moves I might have made and giving no credence to the idea of letting the young grandson win once in a while.

Meanwhile, my grandmother was cooking supper in the small adjoining kitchen.

She was unlike my grandfather to a comical degree—a large, loud, physically powerful woman, the daughter of a farmer and, earlier in their marriage, the work-sharing wife of one. Greeting me, she would shout my name (often going through a roll call in her head of my father's and her son-in-law's and my baby brother's before finally finding mine: *Kenneth! Wayne! Bobby! Dougie!*) and her hugs, I remember, were Greco-Roman moments as she pressed me to her ample bosom, knocking my glasses askew and giving me literally breath-taking squeezes.

Her cacophony of clanging lids and slamming drawers as she cooked made my mother's kitchen manner seem like tranquility itself. Is it valid, or merely facile, to think that the temperamental essences of these two strong women were reflected in the ways they made their great percussive kitchen noises? My mother's seemed, in part, to be deliberate expressions, as if she were mindfully orchestrating them using the instruments at hand, while in contrast, I hear my grandmother's as unscheming, accidental, whatever clatter she caused occurring outside her notice as she hurried clumsily about.

Her nervousness fueled her fretful imagination; she was forever bounding up out of her chair without warning to go check on nothing in particular a room or two away. She held to unfounded opinions and biases that no amount of sensible persuasion could talk her out of. (A teetotaler, she refused to buy Christmas eggnog from the grocery's dairy case because she was convinced there was rum in it.) The scope of her interests—unlike her atlas-reading husband's—did not extend much beyond the day she was living in the room where she was living it. (After hours of needed, drenching, obviously widespread rain she would telephone the farm, four miles away, to ask, "Did you get any rain out there?")

Her vanity was formidable. I picture her monarchal walk down the sanctuary aisle on Sunday morning, nodding left and right and giving little palsied waves. After my grandfather's death roughly a decade after the time I'm remembering, she dyed her hair a russet red, claiming she'd done so somehow accidentally, and frequently repeating that accident for years. Eventually a series of small strokes left her too confused to continue living alone and she moved into the local nursing home. Her room was near the parking lot and main entrance, and she watched from her window with a kind of girlish giddiness, convinced every arriving visitor was coming to call on her. Asked one morning by an aide if she was ready for her shower, she said, oh yes, she was looking forward to it and wondered how many gifts she was going to get.

It was easy as a boy for me to see her as loving and lovable, a daffy, flighty, hilariously opinionated creature; easy, as a boy, to see her only as that.

So the arrangement awaiting my parents and me in 1946 unfolded as planned. We moved down from the apartment to occupy the whole house—the large kitchen; the living room; the dining room; another room, referred to as the playroom, where I kept my books and comic books and toys and costumes.

And my grandparents lived in their little white frame cabin at the north end of Prairie City where the last blocks of the village met someone's fields, and his met someone else's, and so on.

Except that things on our return had *not* quite gone as my parents, or at least my mother, had assumed. After settling back into the upstairs apartment for what they thought would be a short while, they waited almost five years for my grandparents to move into town.

At the late point in her life when we talked about those years, my mother's once complicated anger had become simpler and smaller, much less heavy to hold in her heart. By then she was almost as much the dispassionate historian as the figure in the history. But what she made clear in our talks was her sense at the time, not so much that she and my father had been misled in any deliberate way, but that it actually didn't occur to my grandparents that such an arrangement, extended for so long, would be particularly uncomfortable—our cramped life up above; her in-laws, which is really to say her mother-in-law, presiding below and not about to relinquish any domestic control.

This took the form most notably of her ceaseless advice on how to raise me: why I shouldn't wear dress-up shorts to church; why I had earaches and how to stop them; where to locate the sandbox in the huge backyard so I could be monitored through the windows in case I swallowed something or, my death assured, appeared to be considering climbing a tree. At this remove, her rules and theories sound simply wacky, because they simply were. But my mother was by then, like my grandmother, a stubborn, willful, opinionated woman and, unlike her, a very smart one. So when I look at those days from her point of view—her mother-in-law so relentlessly in her life and she, or so she claimed, feeling she must suppress any words of protest ("I had to bite my tongue!")—when I think of five years of these freighted daily contests, the comedy quickly quiets.

Worse than that, despite her asking my father to speak to his parents, and asking more and more often as time went on, he wasn't able or wasn't willing to say to them, Are you going to buy a house or build one? When are you leaving? You told us you'd be leaving soon after we returned.

Worse still, she came increasingly to feel that the central part of him didn't really want them to.

And, for her, the worst humiliation: the arrangement my father agreed to, allowing us to live in the farmhouse rent-free. But as part of that agreement my grandparents bought and paid for all improvements, every purchase. I don't know if they ever refused a request, and certainly the requests came rarely. But whenever one did—whether for a sofa's new slipcovers, or a room freshly wall-papered, or the wobbly old kitchen table and chairs replaced—my mother had to ask her mother-in-law's permission.

It's easy for me to see things in a more forgiving light. So I can believe that, without considering the implications, my grandparents felt these rent-free, pay-for-nothing conditions were something generous, charitable. What angered my mother as she chafed under them was my father's failure to tell his parents that that's exactly what they were: charity; which meant dependency.

So my parents, owing nothing, owned nothing. Which must have made my mother seem to herself as voiceless as a roomer in what was apparently her house, as powerless as a woman cooking for her bed and board in the kitchen she'd waited five years to occupy; and for what?

With the men's hands and faces scrubbed clean and the food on the table, we all took our usual chairs. Here were the farm's two worlds of work come together—my mother's marvelous food and the men on their dinner-long furlough from the fields. My grandfather sat on my right, my mother on my left, my father directly across from me. I'm embarrassed to say I don't find my baby brother anywhere in this picture, showing I suspect how attentive I was to the presence of the men and their talk, the mysterious diction of field work, which I strained to catch some phrases of.

Many of my classmates who were also farmer's sons, boasting rich vocabularies of plow size and gear boxes and yields per acre, had already begun their field lives. At least they were able to talk as if they had. Listening, ignorant, on school buses and in lunchrooms, I wanted like them to be integral, to have a regular assignment.

At our table, depending on the season, I heard talk of how easily, or not, the earth was turning or where places in the field were still too wet to plant after recent rains or how the combine was behaving after its repair. My mother usually said little, her questions practical and strategic. "Does that mean you'll be working late? When should I plan supper?" But now and then she offered comments that showed she spoke the language passably. She was certainly far closer to fluency than I.

"I saw you out there stopping several times. Is the planter jamming again?"

My problem was twofold. I couldn't help with the harvest, because childhood asthma rendered me seriously allergic to any kind of crop dust and the combine and corn picker moving through the dried and ready rows sent up awful storms of it. Also—and this was apparent early on when my father let me try certain field tasks, sitting behind me on the tractor seat with his hands hovering just above mine as I gripped the steering wheel—I brought a stunning lack of skill to every facet of the work. How to read the tilled soil, for instance; how to distinguish, by the shade and the weave a disk or harrow made in the dirt, where it had passed from where it hadn't; how to smoothly operate a tractor together with the implement it was pulling. Such incompetence ruled out pretty much everything else. Now and then I got to drive a tractor somewhere, pulling a wagon from one field to another. That was about the extent of what I could be trusted to do.

So the most I could do to be a farmer was to eat like one.

Consuming these hot, heavy meals, and with no opportunity to work off the calories through an afternoon of sweat and effort, and with *supper* still to come, I was a fat boy. Not till adolescence did I begin to lose the weight. Photos of me from my portly days invariably show a lad smiling bravely into the camera. The fourth-grade class photo particularly haunts my memory. I'm sitting cross-legged on the floor in the first row, dressed in an ill-advised plaid shirt and my jeans from the Husky section of the boys' department, hunched slightly forward, elbows resting on my thighs; and thus posed, the degree to which my shape is perfectly round is quite remarkable.

I'm not suggesting that I ate like a Cather hired hand to pretend I was a farmer, at least not in any conscious way. After all, my mother's food was damned good. But what I really loved was the rhythm and the ritual of the meal; I loved it for drawing my father and grandfather and their work in from *out there*, in the distance, on the horizon, where just the two of them lived it. At the table, for an hour or so, was as close as I could get to it.

My grandparents' houses, the Bauers' in Prairie City, the Evanses' in Colfax, were six miles apart, the brief distance an easy drive over a wide, straight gravel road, and I have no memory of the four of them ever being under the same roof. This is not to suggest hostility between the families; and my Grandpa and Grandma Evans were both infirm and barely ambulatory when I knew them, he by then blind and crippled, she suffering from severe arthritis, high blood pressure, and obesity. Still, the fact that the families never mixed despite the close proximity does emphasize to me how different they were, the raucous Welsh Evanses, the tidy German Bauers. Growing up, I didn't think anything of it. But after my mother died, while emptying her apartment, I found the newspaper clipping of my parents' wedding I quoted earlier, and I was stopped when I read of the reception at the home of the bride's parents. No matter how singular, how celebratory the occasion, I simply couldn't imagine my father's parents being in my mother's parents' house.

As for *us*—my parents and me and, once he was born, my brother—I don't remember a time when we didn't drive on Sunday to visit Grandma and Grandpa Evans, in that same house, in its same run-down condition, where my mother was raised. The then-gravel road that links the towns traverses rolling, lovely land, the near-hills like soft folds of fabric. In late spring and early summer, my parents looked out their windows as we rode along, assessing the fields. If the emerging rows were full and uniform in their new greenness, my mother pronounced a field "pretty." "Now *there's* a pretty field of beans." Later in the growing season, if that field had been fastidiously weeded, it was even prettier.

Over the years, she'd become increasingly pledged to the Sisyphean task of maintaining a world that was tidy and free of grime. In effect she saw the outdoors as just another room, an extension of the farmhouse, to be kept picked up. From her view out the windows above the long kitchen counter, she lamented the untidiness of nature generally—tree limbs that had fallen in a recent storm, high weeds along the fence line closest to the house. And she brought that same expectation to the appearance of fields, especially our own. Looking out, she was likely to comment to my father (though never in my grandfather's presence) if our neighbor's crop rows looked to be growing more quickly than ours, and if they'd been cleared of buttonweeds and volunteer corn while ours were still waiting to be.

A memory among many: Because she'd never liked the look of the varnished woodwork and baseboards throughout the house, she decided at some point to go room to room, stripping the varnish and painting the woodwork white. In time, the paint began to show cracks, thin as pencil marks, here and there. So she removed the paint where the cracks had appeared, re-sanded the wood, and painted again.

One night, she and I sat watching the *Tonight Show*, as we did every night, my father having gone to bed after fighting to stay awake long enough to watch the news. I was dozing off myself when she suddenly shot forward in her chair and emitted a hard, disgusted "God!" I thought she was responding to something I'd missed that Johnny Carson had said. (Because she often did. When he spoke for comic profit of his "boyhood on the plains of Nebraska," she grew particularly irked. "But you were *born* in Corning, Iowa, Johnny," she would say to the screen, offended,

I think, by what she took as his wish to expunge Iowa from his history.)

But no, that night she rose and walked the length of the room to examine, with an air of sardonic surrender, a hairline fissure that had reappeared in the painted doorframe. She'd been apparently relaxing at the end of the day, watching television with her son, while actually also watching the room where she sat watching. She was poised in her vigilance for the *room* to misbehave.

On our Sunday visits, I saw, besides my grandparents, several aunts and uncles and cousins, all of us come for dinner and the day that stretched wonderfully past supper into mid-evening. There might be ten of us, a dozen, some weeks even more, who came and went, and how the house held us all I can't imagine.

With dinner finished and the dishes cleared, it was usual for my uncles to sit around the kitchen table and talk through the afternoon. As brothers, they were socially unchanged from adolescence—still possessed of that pugilistic verbal spirit that was ready to analyze and argue, to tease and affectionately taunt, as they smoked cigarettes and drank Grain Belt beers through the long hours of afternoon and early evening.

There was Uncle Frank, who loved the big Evans holidays, the Fourth of July most of all, because he loved fireworks, driving each year to Missouri—fireworks were illegal in Iowa—to buy a trunkful for his annual family show. Loved them even though, as a boy, he'd lighted a rocket or a pinwheel or a starburst or something and it blew up in his face and blinded him in his left eye.

There was Uncle Bob, a lifelong bachelor, still living at home, on whose upstairs bedside table I once discovered a stack of paperback pornographic novels, a couple of which I smuggled home and then watched in horror, a few nights later, as my brother drew one from a pocket of my school notebook, saying, "Hey, what's this?" before placing it on the kitchen table where my mother sat helping me with my homework.

Some Sundays, an aged contingent of my grandmother's relatives, four or five cousins she'd grown up with in the south of Wales, arrived unannounced for an afternoon-long visit. My uncles—Frank, Bob, maybe Don the mailman, Bill the butcher, John the Maytag employee—sitting in the kitchen, their own talk drowned out, listening petulantly to the old people in the next room speaking loud, lively Welsh to one another, were unimpressed by their bilingualism, agreeing that the language always sounded to them as though their mother and her cousins were sitting in there competitively hawking up phlegm.

Typically, at some point my uncles' talk turned to sports, and once it did it stayed there for a long while. Of the subjects discussed through the day and evening, it was the one that got them the most animated. They talked of the local high school teams. They talked of the Chicago professional teams, my grandfather's beloved Cubs and the football Bears, whose reputation as notably brutal brutes in a world of them my uncles embraced. They talked about the University of Iowa teams and how intelligently or, more often, ignorantly they were coached. If the hour was after supper, the air by then a cirrus of cigarette smoke, and the usual number of Grain Belt beers had been consumed, the conversation got particularly heated.

"He made the right call, going for the field goal. He's the *coach*, for Christ's sake. He can't *kick* the goddamn ball, too."

"Right call? That bastard couldn't coach a dog to lift his leg."

I can't say whether my own passionate interest in sports was conceived or merely encouraged by listening to my uncles. What I can say is that their conversations stopped me as I passed through the room and caused me to linger at their edge. And I can say that as I listened they gradually taught me a language I discovered I had a natural ear for. At first, I wordlessly took them in, but as I got older and had watched and played more games myself I began to offer my opinions, and, bless my uncles, they were welcomed. I was so happily immersed in this Sunday world of crude communion—of boisterous male population, of my cousins and me playing whatever sport was in season and of me talking about it with my uncles in the kitchen—that it never occurred to me someone might *not* be.

In my memory my father was always treated warmly by the Evanses, and I know how lovingly my grandmother thought of him. But he lacked the quick, sarcastic humor of his brothers-in-law and their eagerness for high, profane debate, the hot argument gene they all possessed. And unlike them, he hadn't been a high school athlete, had no particular knowledge of, no interest in, sports. On rare occasions I persuaded him to play catch, and his motion was a hard, stiff-wristed push, as if he were throwing darts across a very long room. So the hallowed roles of fathers playing catch with sons were reversed: I, returning his tosses with a slightly slowed-down, instructional motion, hoped to teach him by osmosis how to fluidly throw a baseball.

One Sunday afternoon—I was, let's say, eleven or twelve—I stood at the periphery of the table conversation listening to one of my uncles, maybe Uncle Don, the local mailman, strongly offer an opinion, maybe that some quarterback should be benched in favor of another. I remember approaching the table and, standing at my father's shoulder, waiting for a pause and then weighing in. He'd been, as usual, quiet on the subject, which made it even more startling when he turned in his chair and in a low quick hiss said to me that this conversation was for adults, not children, and I'd better leave the kitchen if I couldn't keep my mouth shut.

My uncles' debate was going loudly over his words, which kept them just between the two of us. Stepping away, I was stunned and enraged at the cosmic unfairness of what he'd just said. My uncles had accepted me, invited me in. I'd *been* a part of these conversations for some time now and my father had been sitting right there every Sunday to witness it.

It's plain to me now what wasn't then—that there was a kitchen table at which my father felt an exile, listening to a language he didn't have the ear for. Though his feelings were of course far more complicated than his exclusion for not knowing the Evans lingua franca.

My mistake that day, and maybe his too, was to think that he was angry at *me*.

Finished eating, we sat digesting all that food while my father and grandfather listened to the midday market report on the radio. This went on for what seemed hours. The reader's voice, a recognizably Midwest adenoidal twang absent any inflection, droned on and on, quoting the current and futures prices.

March soybeans.

November hogs.

August wheat.

First from the Chicago mercantile exchange; then, when you thought he was done at last, the news of Omaha's markets.

At the table, my father and grandfather, sipping coffee, listened with the invested concentration I brought to getting the nightly scores.

"Hum," my father might say, after hearing a price.

"Uh-huh," my grandfather might add softly.

For all I know, there could well have been a strategy proposed and responded to in such one-syllable exchanges. For all his gentle shyness, his temperamental deference, my grandfather also possessed real savvy for the commerce of farming. He knew when to buy his seed and when to sell his crop.

December cattle.

October corn.

July sheep.

I understood in the abstract why this market news was important, which made it no less tedious to listen to. But I disliked it not just because it was so deadly boring. Watching my father and grandfather and their close attention to the monotonous stream of numbers, I could sense almost tangibly their thoughts beginning to move away from the table and back into their exclusive life.

When at last the man on the radio was done, which a part of me wanted and a part of me didn't, my father looked up at the wall clock. "Well, Dad, what do you say?" And with that, they pushed back their chairs.

My grandfather once again thanked my mother for another delicious dinner.

"You're welcome, Dad," she said. I hear her voice in this passing of pleasantries as undefended and warm. Years later, when we talked about the difficulties of this period of her life, she said that she loved him, too, her father-in-law; that she felt he was a kind and lovely man.

And yet, his aura of calm, his preference for the solitude of fields, away from the obligations of talk, alert instead to the language of the land—all of that which was endearing about him also kept him from thinking, or allowed him not to think, about the terms of tenancy at the core of my mother's unhappiness.

I wonder if her frustration came as well from her starting to feel the limitations generally of life as a wife and young mother on a family farm in Iowa. She'd been on her own in the world at the age of nineteen, a teacher presiding in the proverbial one-room schoolhouse, driving country roads to work and home and wherever else her beloved sagging-chassis Model A took her. I don't believe she now saw her old life through a lens of memory that was hopelessly distorted; only that she remembered it as work she had liked very much and had been getting very good at. That she saw it as a life that had been *hers*.

I believe the primitive poverty of my mother's childhood left an indelible mark on her. That living now so near her family, spending at least one long day a week, often more, in the house whose dereliction had been remarkably preserved, hardened her desire not to re-create the noise and landscape of her growing up. And don't we all either repeat or repudiate that noise, that landscape?

I can't imagine the complexity of the pull she felt and the rewards she got from all those years of weekly family gatherings. For me, it was simple; it was the delight of knowing—after days of well-scrubbed solitude on the farm, especially in summer when there wasn't school—that Sunday was the day life was lived. The other six were passed in variations of waiting for it.

My grandparents' house had not been improved in its comforts and conveniences from the way my mother knew it when she was growing up with her six brothers and two sisters. It still had no hot water and no indoor plumbing. The sources of heat were two coal-burning stoves, one in the kitchen, a second in the living room, which meant the upstairs bedrooms were Icelandic in winter. Given my grandmother's physical limitations, much of the housecleaning was left to my older cousins, Bill and Jim, the orphaned sons of her daughter Dorothy, dead from cancer at thirty, who lived with my grandparents. So contagions of dust balls skipped like tiny tumbleweeds along the dirty wooden floors, over the cracked linoleum in the kitchen. When I entered the downstairs bedroom to toss my coat on the bed, I held my breath against the possibility that my grandfather's chamber pot had not recently been emptied, though I suspect my anticipation of that smell made it, while real enough, even worse than it was. This was not the case outdoors, where imagination could not exaggerate the stench in the deep, dark confines of the outhouse. Suffocatingly hot in summer and numbingly cold in winter, a shock to your privates when you dropped your jeans, the outhouse stood at the edge of the backyard just before the weedy alley, which made it easy for Halloween revelers to come along undetected and knock it over, revealing the next morning to all the world the rectangular hole over which the structure sat, a craggy geology of old and older turds. The annual tipping of the outhouse was an event that we, the younger cousins, never tired of and we'd gather around, half a dozen of us, sometimes more, and peer down into the hole, utterly repulsed. Being utterly repulsed was of course the whole idea. Then we'd watch Uncle Bob and cousins Bill and Jim tip the outhouse back up and into place. A kind of Amish barn-raising moment, in its way.

Cousin Jim was my favorite, four years older than I, handsome and funny and an exceptional athlete. Growing up, I awarded him an immaculate heroism, until the day we stood outside idly chatting and I heard an unmistakable click, click as he absently flicked the lid of the cigarette lighter in a front pants pocket. Click, click. The sound suggested to me something close to switch-blade delinquency, which made Jim suddenly no longer pure, and therefore even more compelling.

On Sunday, we played in the big backyard that had been the enormous town-lot-sized vegetable garden. My grandparents had been pioneering locavores by necessity. Or we got fabulously filthy playing "avalanche" in the coal shed, after which we took sponge baths in the little unheated room attached to the kitchen, standing in a tub of water heated on the propane cooking stove, and in bathing we unknowingly mimicked the archival ritual of Grandpa's nightly toilette on returning from the mines.

At night, after supper, we devised games and pranks. For a time, our favorite involved my brother, the youngest cousin, who at three, perhaps four, was still a prodigious drooler, wet spots big as bibs on the front of his shirts. We sneaked him upstairs to the dark, unheated bedrooms, where a louvered register in the linoleum floor allowed the rising heat from below to warm the frigid space. At least in theory. There, we instructed him to lie down with his face over the open register, then waited, patient as ice fishermen, for an adult to pass beneath. Nothing symbolizes the magical crude universe of my grandparents' house so well.

What was generally seen as, at best, socially unpleasant—*Bobby, wipe your chin. Bobby, close your mouth*—became on Sunday a marvelous weapon. *Ready Bobby? Drool!*

So this world was a primitively permissive place, wonderfully soiled and malodorous and filled with a clannish liveliness that somehow relied on, somehow got its strength from, that crudeness. The family decay a kind of compost. It was where exuberant life resided naturally with grime and dust and my grandparents' dramatic bodily decline, and in my child's view there was nothing incompatible in any of this.

As for my mother, I remember the tone of her voice on Sunday as she urged me to hurry and change from my church clothes to my jeans, to find my baseball glove right *now* and get into the car so we could drive those quick ten miles. However complex her reasons, she was as impatient to get there as I was.

Perhaps she was able to stay attentive to the life she'd rejected because it helped her see herself in such sharp contrast to it, to remind her of her progress away from the vigorous squalor of her childhood. And I suspect, most vital of all, she also got a kind of weekly replenishment, that she needed to feel the regular recovery of some old vivacity that was there, in that house, with the dust and decay.

So her weekly returns were ones she was able to make eagerly because she had her compensatory world ten miles away, where she'd set the terms and tone of its domesticity, and where, if liveliness brought some messiness with it, she wasn't interested.

I think, when she began to date my father seriously, an impulse in her felt she could have the liveliness of life without the mess. I believe she saw him in their first years as the handsome blade he was, who perfectly combined the rascality of the Evanses with none of the squalor. But once they were home from the war and took off their costumes, the unwelcome surprises of her adult life began, and she got angry at them and stayed that way. However understandable, however justified that anger—and I believe at the start and to a real extent it was—my mother held on to it from that time on until the last years of her life.

In something like the way she judged the fields, she became more generally a monitor of our daily lives. Of my brother's and mine, certainly; but mostly of our father's; mostly of him and his, by far. In Katherine Anne Porter's great story "The Journey," an old woman long unhappy in her marriage remembered her husband and "mourned him with dry eyes angrily." Could this be said of my mother—that every moment of her judgment of my father could also be seen as a perverse act of mourning? That she mourned the loss of the man she'd fallen in love with, while she worked without pause to make that man disappear? That she grieved the husband she no longer had and resented the one she demanded he become, his spirit growing steadily less recognizable compared to the one that had caught her heart?

I think of him sitting at the table with his brothers-in-law and, turning to me, telling me to butt out. If I was the age, give or take a year, that I'm quite sure I was, he would have been not even forty, his personality at a relatively early stage of its alteration. Even so, the contrast is dramatic when I imagine the young man who gallivanted with his cronies and posed with them in his vested suits, who courted my mother and was eager to marry and guided her smoothly and considerately around the Val Air Ballroom dance floor. That young man had also sat at the Evans kitchen table and was surely confident enough, if the talk turned to sports or some other subject he had no knowledge of, to smile and say and know he was saying it in a way that would be charming, *Who cares? Let's talk about anything else.*

When I think of that young man, I wonder if, at the moment my father snapped at me, he was thinking of him, too.

Every day, I followed my father and grandfather out of the kitchen, accompanying them down the sidewalk, through the gate, and for some thirty yards more through patches of barnyard grass, mid-thigh high, until we reached the two tractors. I filled them both with gasoline from the big tank resting on its high wooden platform. Next I guided the crank that started my grandfather's ancient Case into the hole below the radiator at the nose of the tractor. Then, with the crank ready, I stepped away and my grandfather stepped in, for I wasn't strong enough to turn it with the necessary force. He frequently assured me the issue wasn't so much my lack of strength; I was plenty strong enough. I just needed to get a feel for the precise leverage, for the crank's proper angle of engagement. This of course was a lie.

As he set himself, I studied him, noting his position and posture, like a boy being shown the proper way to throw a baseball. He seemed to take a conjuring moment, then with what I saw as an effortless flick of his wrist he gave the crank a single turn and the tractor belched reverberantly, as if from a huge meal, into life.

I watched the two of them mount. My grandfather as always rode sidesaddle, his rod-stiff leg making it impossible for him to sit conventionally. Then the tractors eased away like horses from a hitching rail, or so they seemed to me. I waved to them as they headed back out. Picturing that moment now, I give myself a sweeping, semaphorical gesture, as mawkish in memory's eye as the boy standing in the dusty street waving good-bye to Shane.

When my mother and I talked about those years, she said, "Your grandpa was the love of your dad's life. When he died it absolutely broke his heart and no one, sure not me, could be a replacement. And the truth of it is, your dad didn't want anyone to."

Though I obviously can't know how completely this was true, it was clear how completely she believed it was. My father would have had his story, his version, of course. But this was hers, and she blamed my grandfather—a man she loved for being lovely—for none of it; though it should be remembered that he strongly urged my father to join him in the life. Yes, I'm sure he'd loved the idea and subsequently loved the dailiness of farming with his son. But then again, he loved farming.

And I recall a conversation my father and I once had about his father beckoning him back to Iowa to be his partner. As he talked of it, the invitation was one he didn't think about very long before accepting. And, he continued, it was one he was never tempted to offer me in turn. For obvious reasons, as I've said—I'd amply demonstrated my unsuitability for farming—but also, he told me, because he himself needed a while to find his feelings for it; that for a time he performed a job he was dispassionately very good at. His tremendous competence, then, was a curse in the beginning and eventually a blessing, but he didn't want to put me in anything like the same position—to have to *work* to love the life.

Still, as my mother saw it, she was feeding her competition in a contest she shouldn't have had to enter, one she was certain she couldn't win. But as a boy, I knew nothing, suspected nothing, of what all was being wordlessly passed around the noonday table, the many portions and flavors that were being shared.

Leaving the barnyard and starting back toward the house, the men and their tractors no longer in view, I assign myself the chore of joining her—a short, pretty woman in her early thirties, wearing a housedress of printed cotton and summer sandals—to help her wash and dry the dishes. It seems only right that I should aid her in this twice-daily domestic task, given everything she served me, and everything she labored not to.

After her death, when I'd done what I could to clear her apartment, I drove away from Prairie City, headed west. I was traveling all the way to Northern California, to the town of Sonoma, where my partner, Sue, and I would be spending some months mercifully away from the Boston winter. I'd be driving all the way on Interstate 80, the country's great latitudinal belt, until I ran out of continent. Following that route, how could I not stop in Cheyenne?

There'd been an extraordinary snowstorm, the latest in a winter of them, while I was in Iowa, and traveling the state's western half I saw drifts, great rolling berms and mesas of snow, on both sides of the highway. Tucked into and poking out of them were countless abandoned cars and trucks, some nose-down in the drifts, some tipped on their sides, some steeply angled in snow banks with their headlights looking skyward, four or five or six of them every mile, so many I felt I was passing through an eerie postapocalyptic stillness. When I later described this scene to my brother on the phone, he explained that law now forbids all towing after nightfall. So what looked like the aftermath of some panicked exodus was a few days' worth of spinouts and collisions that hadn't yet been cleared, which made the spectacle no less impressive to me.

To reach Cheyenne, I had of course to travel the breadth of Nebraska, the legendarily empty and endless Nebraska of Cather's fiction and my parents' saga. Remembering her descriptions and theirs, I was braced for expanses so vast, a flatness so unvarying, as to make a fine prairie hallucination. I found instead as I drove that while Nebraska is indeed wide and empty, and much of it table-flat, I didn't feel the stunning sameness of landscape, made more uniform still by an evenly applied coat of snow gleaming in the sun, that I'd been braced to find and pronounce unendurable.

I remember two completely unrelated things that stood out in my drive across Nebraska. Early on, I watched a pickup traveling in my direction at my speed along a local road paralleling the interstate. In the back of the truck stood an especially enormous Newfoundland, standing still as a statue against the onrushing winter wind. The dog was majestic, triumphant, commanding, regal, as it rode in absolutely perfect stillness. It seemed as if it were being driven to some canine land of adoring subjects.

And the second thing: the next day, near the state's western border, I looked over into a field and saw a weathered hand-lettered wooden sign that read, "Jesus (hearts) Sodomy." For the next several miles I pondered the narrative that had resulted in the sign—how it had come to be erected, and by whom, and in what mood? Were they vigilante ironists? Were they sincere Nebraska gays? And how had it continued to stand—its wind-blistered surface suggested it had been there a *while*—in a field by a fence line in bright-red-state Nebraska? These are the sort of moments that strike and stay with you when you're moving alone through high-gloss white monotony.

And then I was in Wyoming, and not long after that, at the tourist center on the outskirts of Cheyenne. The winter landscape I'd been driving through was deceptive, for the temperature had been getting increasingly warm as I drove west. Just *how* warm I hadn't appreciated. When I got out of the car, Cheyenne greeted me with a temperature of seventy-three degrees and blue skies. I simply stood beside the car, feeling the warmth and, with it, slightly vertiginous as I took in the unblemished skies at 6100 feet above sea level. It was freakish bliss after many mean weeks of snow and ice.

Inside the tourist center, I told the friendly guide I was looking for Van Lennen Street.

Sure, she said, she knew just where it was and assured me it was easy to find. She unfolded a map of the little city—53,000 people, and Wyoming's largest—and drew a simple route with her felt-tipped pen into the center of town. Her thick black line made a right turn, proceeded some six or seven blocks, then turned left onto Van Lennen.

"Easy," she repeated.

Back in the car, I spread the map out on the seat beside me and headed in to find the house where my parents lived when I was born.

After blocks of gas stations, franchise restaurants, convenience shops, the usual detritus of chain-store commerce, I found, as easily as promised, Van Lennen and turned left. I rolled the window down and drove very slowly on the suddenly quiet residential street. The neighborhood was a bit down on its heels, its small wooden bungalows, variously shabby, standing close to one another in their scruffy yards.

I continued to drive along at a crawl, simply taking in the street while searching for house numbers, and had driven four or five blocks when 2008 appeared on my left. I pulled to the curb, shut off the engine, and looked across the street at a large frame house painted lime-sherbet green and surrounded on three sides by patches of weedy lawn. There was a realtor's "For Sale" sign out front.

Comparing it to the house in photos my mother had kept, I saw that it had been made considerably larger. Box-shaped additions had been added on both sides, making it a bulky triptych. It appeared structurally relaxed, as if some of its joints, like some of mine, no longer held together quite as securely as they had. On the left a set of wooden stairs climbed to a second-story door. Judging from the many mailboxes out front, it was now a rooming house.

I turned my attention to a window to the right of the front steps. It looked unchanged in size and shape from its appearance in snapshots—some of them showing either my mother or my father holding me, the rag-doll-malleable newborn wearing a knit skullcap, while standing next to that first-floor window. On one of the photos, my mother had written, with an arrow pointing to it, "Our apartment."

I got out of the car and crossed the street and stood on the sidewalk a short distance from the front steps. In maybe half a dozen photos from my mother's cache she's sitting on those steps, dressed for the season, alone, or with a friend, or, in one, with a young man in uniform, a pipe jutting at a jaunty angle from his mouth, presumably an Army buddy of my father's. None of the photos include my father, no doubt the picture taker. Individual as they are, there's a consistency running through them, a particular quality in her achingly young smile, a kind of sly buoyancy, which I attribute to her certainty that she's smiling not only for the moment, but for all the reasons and occasions she'll be smiling in the future. Now, looking at the steps in front of me, rebuilt from those she sat on or entirely replaced, I saw her sitting there smiling that smile.

Standing there, I realized I was waiting to be emotionally transported. There I was, having made a kind of pilgrimage to the spot where I began. Shouldn't I be taken by the import of the instant—moved, if not to tears, at least to a lump in the throat, by the profound significance of having found my way on a divinely warm and sunny January day to this ramshackle, accidental monument to me? Maybe the search had been too easy: into town, a right turn, then a left, and a few blocks later there it was. Maybe I should act out the scene more fully—walk up to the door and firmly knock and when the bemused occupant answers (it's mid-morning, it's a weekday, and who knocks on doors these days but Greenpeace militants and Christly solicitors?), say what the character in the scene always says: *Sorry to bother you, but, well, I used to live here. Would you mind if I came in and looked around for just a second?*

So I wasn't transported; I wasn't moved. I felt no powerful emotional surge. It wasn't that I felt detached from what I was standing before. I was simply extremely interested, my eye canvassing the scene for the physical details—the weedy lawn, the two-by-six wooden railing—to visually memorize and take with me as immeasurably meaningful historical souvenirs. Yes, that was it. I was attentive; more than that, I was absorbed, in the way we absorb the details of an historical site—the slope of the land down to the creek, or the shade of velvet upholstery on the couch—that particularly fascinates us. As for histories, it was only technically where *mine* began. But, in all the ways that mattered to what they started and what they lost, it was absolutely where my parents' had.

When I'd gotten all my mind could hold, and taken a roll of

snapshots with one of those cardboard Kodak cameras I'd bought at a convenience store, I left the car parked on Van Lennen and spent the next few hours walking around town. Everywhere I looked, as I passed through neighborhoods, sat in tree-shaded parks, I pictured them. I put them on park benches. I sat them in old, sleazy-faced cafes. I slowly strolled, a short distance from their apartment, along the prime commercial streets where I hoped I might spot the front where the Montgomery Ward department store had stood, the backdrop for my mother and the other clerks when they posed in cowgirl regalia. The four or five blocks I walked along were lively; the western-style and brick storefronts on Capitol Avenue were well kept. The open skies seemed to fill the vacant lots between the stores, creating a visual deception that the buildings and stores were merely flat facades. And my mother's department store could have been any one of them. The huge marquee of the Lincoln Theater might have been the one in the background of my mother's cowgirls photo.

I decided as I walked, and stopped for coffee, and walked again, that this was the perfect place for them to be living away from rural Iowa for the first time, allowing them to feel both comfortable and new. It was a city, but a very small one, not a place that would have initially overwhelmed them. The nearness of the bungalow neighborhoods to the streets of commerce. The physical intimacy of its layout, with the capitol building, a marble structure of real but modest grandeur, like a county courthouse, only a few blocks from their apartment. And all of it set in a landscape of grasses and low bluffs, satisfyingly strange to their Midwestern sense of terrain, but still relatively flat, set in foothills, the panorama of Wyoming's raw mountain drama farther west. The temperature had begun to drop as I walked back to Van Lennen Street. I took a last look at the house, then got into the car and drove away from Cheyenne, heading west again.

In less than an hour, climbing three thousand feet to higher altitude, I met snow, which quickly turned into a storm, falling ever more fiercely until it was a pointillist white screen I couldn't see beyond, finally reaching an intensity that forced the interstate to close. It often does in high-country Wyoming in winter. Set up along the highway just after each exit is a tower-tall version of those railroad crossing arms that descend and block the road while a flashing sign orders you back to the town you just passed.

The town I'd just passed was Rock Springs, and there I spent the next two days in a Holiday Inn, waiting out the storm and replaying in my mind the afternoon I'd spent getting to know my parents when they and their marriage were young and healthy.

I'd seen the places, the spots where they'd lived and gathered with friends, the house, the stores, the streets, where they were vibrantly naïve. I'd gotten to imagine them when they were kids.

As I thought about the afternoon, the question I felt forming was the one I have still. Whether I should feel sadness that the life I toured one afternoon lasted so briefly, or instead feel glad that they had it at all, a time they could, and did, recall for the rest of their lives? For it wasn't just a wish or a dream they conjured. They could remember years they'd actually lived—so much better than a wish or a dream, because a memory gave them an emotional capital they could draw on without its principal ever being reduced.

The first night at the Rock Springs Holiday Inn, I was walking down the hall, returning to my room after supper in the dreadful hotel restaurant, when I felt my heart suddenly begin to beat too earnestly. It had been acting this way for a while now, beginning suddenly to pound with no warning and seemingly from no cause.

I'd gone to see a cardiologist, who'd assigned me to wear a heart monitor for twenty-four hours. When we met to discuss the monitor's results, he explained a condition called tachycardia, a kind of electrical short-circuiting of the heart. He prescribed a modest dosage of a beta blocker, a drug that works to stop heart cells from misfiring.

Back in my hotel room, I felt my heart continuing to race. And I wondered whether it was working too strongly from anxiety that had tardily kicked in after driving through the extraordinary snowstorm? Or was it from spending a day in a false summer sun tracing, inventing, watching my parents move about in their magical past? Or was it caused, instead, by a simple hitch of cardiology that had nothing to do with feelings, with emotions, with anything that qualifies as a matter of the heart? If that was the case—and I knew rationally it was—then what was the heartless impulse in my heart that the beta blocker had not been able to block? And how much better to think of the heart—mine; my mother's; my father's; anyone's—pounding, pulsing, refusing the cadence of its stolid, steady rhythm, because it was frightened, or broken, or desperately thrilled.

IOWA WINE

ᔓ

WALKING THROUGH THE VINEYARD, I RAISED MY EYES TO the top of the vines and saw new pale-green tendrils corkscrewing toward the sun. Their reaching for light was, of course, natural tropism. But if grape vines had a conscience (and I've heard winemakers in Napa and Sonoma sometimes speak of them as if they do—a conscience, a brain, and a resolute will) then their trying to get still taller at that point in the season could also be seen as greedy and thoughtless. For the good of the harvest, it was time they were sending their energy back down to the clusters of grapes holding on below. But the vines and their berries are natural competitors for the carbohydrates and the minerals and the needed nutrients, and it's a competition the grapes can't win on their own. So human beings have to intervene, men passing through to snip the selfish tendrils.

The vineyard I was visiting on that hot July afternoon was a postcard-perfect eight-acre lot planted on a subtly sloping hillside. And among the pleasures I felt as I moved along between the rows was an atavistic one. I was in a kind of intimate trance, something not unlike my childhood state of mind when I escaped into whatever invented world I was living in that day—the jungle explorer, the sheriff tracking the outlaw in the woods—as I walked stealthily through a jungle, or a forest, depending, of harvest-high corn.

As it happens, this is a fitting comparison. For when I reached the end of that vineyard and stepped again into full sunlight the first thing I saw was a grain silo rising huge and royal-blue on the near horizon; and then, panning right, across the gray ribbon of gravel road, a lush patchwork of complementary greens: corn and soybean fields running infinitely. What I was viewing was true and not some hallucinatory blurring of memory and moment. But because I'd been deep in the Zen of tall rows I needed a few seconds to reorient myself, as I did when, a boy, I emerged from my father's field to confront the vista of farmhouse and barnyard I'd escaped for a time. Simply put, standing in the shade of the leafy end vines and taking in the familiar rural terrain, I couldn't yet quite believe there were vineyards in Iowa.

I'd read that there were, some months earlier, in a front-page story in the *New York Times*. The piece had predictable fun with the idea of colliding cultures: the Midwest farmer, plain in his tastes, indeed shy to admit to appetites of any sort, his simple mood and attitude honed by the work and the weather; and, against that, the sun-blessed winemaker, the festive sophisticate, believing life is a thing to savor openly and consume until you're full. Like all stereotypes, these are gross caricatures. It's also true that I've found enough in them to send me fleeing from the first and seeking versions of the latter for most of my adult life.

Our farm was four miles from Prairie City, then a village of eight hundred people, and because I performed well in its classrooms and passably on its athletic fields, my school years were rewarding and socially easy. But I learned early on that I had no gift for farming. My mistakes at the wheel of a tractor are too many to list and too astounding to be believed. I could tell you, for instance, about confusing the position of first gear and reverse and driving up onto and nearly over a plow. But even beyond the farcical failures, a more general feeling steadily came to me about the Midwest farming life and my place in it—that I was a stranger in a culture whose ambition was for a kind of grand inelegance, a determined plainness. By adolescence, I knew—simply and ever more comfortably knew—that whatever my future, it would be somewhere away.

The winding route I've taken doesn't matter here except as an itinerary that leads to the moment of my stepping from the newly planted Iowa vineyard and viewing the verdant scenery of my past. So, quickly: my first city was Chicago, where I found that I wanted to live in cities, for the same reasons that anyone who wants to live in them does, for the chance to take some of their energy, to feel myself inside the pattern, the splendid shifts and tumbling of their kaleidoscopic life. With brief detours, I've lived in cities since, thinking myself forever on the lam from the order and the ordinances of the farm.

But at a point within this happy urban history, I also discovered the California wine country. Driving north from San Francisco more than thirty years ago to visit a friend in the Sonoma valley, the hills in autumn the tawny shade of a lion's hide, I sensed myself moving through a landscape that immediately drew me in as no open terrain ever had. Still, some years of city life passed before I returned, this time with my wife, and after that we went back again and again, sometimes for a week, sometimes for a working month or two. Finally, a decade ago, we bought a home in the hills above Sonoma. For a few years, I felt incredibly lucky to live there half the time, until the impossibility of maintaining a dauntingly expensive bicoastal life became readily apparent, as it should have before we bought the house. With great reluctance, after five years, we sold it.

I know my feeling for that part of the world is hardly unique. But *as* a feeling, *for* a particular geography, it's unique for me. In thinking about it over the years, in asking myself why, I concluded long ago that it mostly had to do with the culture's unhesitant embrace of daily pleasures, for its ordinary ceremonies of making and tasting (see cartoon description of winemaker above). In other words, for a cadence of life that was as far as I could get from the seasons and solemnities of my home place.

When the *Times* was finished being amused at the fact that there were farmers in Iowa growing grapes instead of corn, the paper's wine critic, Eric Asimov, got around to tasting some of the wines. After dismissing most of them as the syrup of summer coolers, he wrote that one producer in particular, Jasper Winery, using grapes I'd never heard of—Chancellor and St. Croix, Noiret and Marechal Foch—was actually making "enjoyable and distinctive wines," that Jasper's red blend was "juicy and pleasing with a floral spice," and that its red varietal, compared to the blend, was "a little more polished, if not as exuberant."

But how could this be? Wine grapes need a climate of splendid monotony: brief winters of rain giving to steady sun. Day after day of dry heat and cool nights. And as for the soil, grapevines produce best when consigned to rock and gravel that require their roots to work, "to build their muscles," as I once heard a Napa winemaker put it, a grunting and straining that gives the grapes their balance of substance and sweetness. In other words, a partnership of weather and earth that has nothing in common with the seasonal climate the Midwest hopes for—a lavishing of sun and showers through the months of spring and summer—and the brutal winters it typically endures. And nothing in common either with its rich, black, anciently wind-sifted loam. Given these drastic differences, how could anyone make "exuberant," "polished," distinctively enjoyable wines in Iowa?

Within all I hadn't known and couldn't fathom about any of this, I was certain of one thing. That the estate vineyard of Jasper Winery, described in the *Times* as just outside the town of Newton, was less than ten miles from the corn and soybean farm where I was raised.

Driving to the winery from Prairie City, I followed the narrow blacktop I traveled with my parents and younger brother countless times growing up. The undulating countryside was a high-summer green, the color that most flatters Iowa's features. Approaching a particular farm a couple of miles out of town that my parents predictably admired as we passed—the neatness of the barnyard, the land's ideally gradient slope—I looked over to see a sight too thematically perfect, except that it *was* what I saw: the plot next to the house was a recently staked vineyard.

Jean Groben runs the daily business of Jasper Winery; her husband, Paul, a physician, manages to find some hours to help oversee the vineyards when he's not with patients; and in its way the story of their winery perfectly captures the farmer's dual temperament, one that combines a clinician's interest in all the agronomy with the mystic's whimsy required for putting something in the ground and assuming it will live.

The Grobens had long been ambitious gardeners, and they were keenly interested in cooking and wine. It followed, then, that they might notice the growing number of Midwest wineries and, intrigued, begin to research the essential subject. Grapes.

What they learned was that others were intrigued, too. Scientists at Cornell and the University of Minnesota were experimenting with French-American hybrids that would be ornery enough to take the climate and accommodating enough so that their juices, first in tanks and after that in barrels, would let the stems and the skins and then new oak complicate their taste.

So the Grobens decided to plant a vineyard. They had land behind their lovely country home. Now they knew what grapes they needed. The only thing missing was someone to make the wine.

"When I left here after high school, I never dreamed I'd end up back in Newton." Mason Groben, Jean and Paul's son, confessed this as we rode in his pickup the few miles from the vineyard we'd been walking to the winery back in town. He's a handsome, square-faced young man, with close-cropped hair and an athlete's prominently bridged nose. As he drove he spoke of *his* winding route away from Iowa. His was thirty years shorter than mine and it got him to the wine country more directly than mine did, but he arrived at about the age I was when I drove up from San Francisco that sublime early autumn afternoon. In fact, he was working at a winery in Sonoma County and thinking he might like to make his life at it when his parents called him with a proposal. They would send him to the University of California, Davis, where most everyone who's serious about it goes to study viticulture, if he would bring what he learned back to Iowa with him.

He said he knew his parents were planning to enjoy themselves at their new venture, but that they also wanted to make the best wine possible, using modern steel holding tanks and expensive oak barrels. Given that, and with the interest he already had, the opportunity was too attractive to resist.

As I rode the rural highway with Mason Groben and listened to him speak of his surprise at finding himself back in the home-town he was certain he'd left for good, I indulged in some goofy, revisionist history. Mixing it all together—my past and that moment with Groben and the daily life that has drawn me—I asked myself what might have happened if the kind of farming Iowa has done since the prairie grasses were cleared was instead what a very small share of it has begun to be. What if my father had asked me to stay and make wine? This was, as I say, sheer romance that required a complete recasting, starting with the not incidental truth that my father hated wine. Pure make-believe then. Except for that part of me—surely a part of us all—that has wanted, and will always want despite the evidence, what I do most competently and feel most deeply to be the skills and sensibility of the place where I began. And so, as Mason Groben drove us toward his winery, I glanced over at him and let myself imagine I was looking at the farmer I might have had the chance to be.

ॐ

Mason told me as we drove that his family had bought a larger building for a planned increase in production, from four thousand to ten thousand cases over the next five years, and as we pulled up to the winery it was clear why they had. It was a neat red building with a sloping roof, and scarcely bigger than the shed where my father kept his two tractors and assorted field implements. It sat at the north edge of Newton, three blocks from the Maid-Rite Diner, where our family occasionally drove for special summer suppers, giving my mother a night away from a hot kitchen, and which continues to thrive, listing, among the side dishes on its menu, "bowl of meat." (Let me say that I love the diner's signature sandwich—loose ground beef, steamed and moist and seasoned with salt and pepper, piled high on a hamburger bun and served with mustard and onions and dill pickles and a spoon for what the bun can't hold and a history of permissive summer evenings too hot to ask anyone to cook.)

Inside, Mason showed me the cramped but gleaming-clean space that held the steel tanks, the oak barrels stacked on racks, and then we moved into the adjoining sales shop. It felt cozy and informal, despite its retail purpose, not because it was so small but because Mason's mother, Jean Groben, so warmly presides.

She is a fair, slender woman, quick to laugh, emanating a great, friendly energy that had to come in handy when you were starting a winery—anywhere, of course, but especially in the midst of a population that was new to what you were making and un-practiced at buying it. She had bottles of Jasper wines arranged and ready along the tiny tasting bar at the back of the room. The pleasantly juicy, floral-spiced red blend. The more polished if less exuberant Cherry Creek Chancellor. Also a white made from Seyval Blanc grapes, and, finally, two rosés. As she poured, she offered the story of how and why Jasper began, that history of her and her husband's interests I alluded to. And then the three of us ritualistically commenced. We swirled the Chancellor and lowered our noses like hummingbirds to the nectar of scent and swirled the wine some more and watched it runnel silkily down the sides of our glasses. Finally, we took sips.

For the record, Jasper's Cherry Creek Chancellor tasted to me pleasingly similar to what wine folks call an "approachable" cabernet, nothing especially layered and lingering, but with a lovely hovering of vanilla at the top of the scent and with none of the chalkiness of some young Bordeaux. In other words, it tasted remarkably good. By which I mean—given Mason Groben's challenge, given the newness of the grape and the newness of the venture and all there was to learn about them both—it tasted, remarkably, good.

But my first response had little to do with the nuances of its nose or the flavors unfolding as it traveled my tongue, no features I can speak of in terms of tannins or mouthfeel, a vernacular as strange to me as the language of the land and how to tend it— "eight bottom plows" and "over / under hydraulic"—that I heard spoken in the school cafeteria and left me, a failed rural linguist, sitting mute and ignorant.

Instead, what I tasted in the wine initially were the marvelous flavors of pride and relief. It was nothing the wine released but what the first taste of it released in me. It was so familiar, that feeling, a defensive protection as natural as tropism, as complex as an aged vintage, and one that flares whenever someone takes condescending aim at that easy Midwest caricature: the one that drew the *Times* to wryly report the story of Iowa wine; the one that I have so often traded on to say—to anyone around me, yes, but mostly to myself—that I'm separate from it.

I asked Mason how much of his master's education he was able to use in his work.

He said, "What I learned helps me a lot with the *making* of the wine. But the growing of it, that's been pretty much learning on the job." No one at UC Davis had, while he was there, a lot of pertinent advice for growing the grapes Jasper grows in Midwest weather in Midwest soil.

He told me, for example, that the Iowa earth is so robustly nutrient that the grapes he used to make a Riesling-style white grew too quickly, too profusely, so he had to pick them early and then add sugar in the tanks to raise the sweetness, the brix count, to a level they would have developed naturally if they behaved on the vines the way UC Davis said grapes behaved.

He said he was especially challenged in making his reds because even those grapes, which were bred to stand the Midwest climate, would like to get more sustained dry weather, more uninterrupted sun, than they do. "This year's been unusual," he said. "All the farmers have been complaining about the lack of rain." He smiled, a bit sheepishly I thought, and admitted, "But that's been great for us."

We'd been tasting our way along the row of wines, Jean pouring, and finally reached the two rosés. The first of them Mason worked with commitment to define. The second he made frankly to sell as widely as possible.

We tried the first. Once again I tasted native pride, a light but full-flavored tartness, and I admired the deep cherry-pink color. Then Jean Groben poured us tastes of the second. "You'll definitely be able to tell the grape in this one," she said, smiling.

Again, in unison, we lowered our noses and I got an overpowering smell of grape juice.

Jean laughed. "We call it our breakfast wine," she said, and it was true that in a food and wine pairing it might have matched best with Kellogg's Corn Flakes. She said, "When Mason complains about making it, I remind him it's the sales from this one that let him make his estate Chancellor."

Mason smiled and shrugged. Alas.

The shop door opened and a customer entered. Jean enthusiastically welcomed him to Jasper. He was a small, thin man in summer short-sleeves and khakis. He paused, seeming momentarily confused, as if he'd been given wrong directions. But after looking around at the wines arranged for sale on countertops, he walked back and joined us at the tasting bar. He pointed to the thimbles of "breakfast" rosé in the bottoms of our glasses and said he'd have whatever we were drinking.

Jean took a glass from the rack and poured a taste of breakfast wine and he immediately knocked it back, a movie-western gesture, a thirsty varmint at the bar. "Not bad," he said, and I almost expected him to wipe the back of his hand across his mouth, like Gabby Hayes. "Got anything a little sweeter?"

The first time my wife and I rented a house in Sonoma, more than twenty years ago, we thought it would be a fine idea to invite my parents to visit for a week. And it was. Neither of them had been to California and they enjoyed themselves immensely, charmed by the historic town square, delighted by the annual harvest festival, the wine country's version of a Midwest county fair, where the wineries come together to offer samplings of the season. My father, a beer drinker who, as I said, did not like wine, was especially pleased to see that you were *supposed* to spit it into a bucket, which he proceeded to do with great glee, moving from booth to booth and taking aim like a mischievous boy given an evening's dispensation.

But through the week, as we meandered the back roads taking in the scenery, what I wasn't hearing from him was any comment on the beauty of the landscape, that arid, blond-grass lushness dotted with the greens of live oaks and madrones, the same hills in the same season that had immediately compelled me. With each day I felt myself growing increasingly annoyed with his silence, as you do when you're waiting for an opinion that matters to you, the spoken approval of something or someone you've fallen in love with.

Until, as we wound through the country toward a picnic site one afternoon, my father slightly shook his head and said, "I've been thinking all week, man oh man, they sure been hit by the drought out here."

I'm sorry to say that what I heard just then was a parochial failure to see the natural magnificence around him. I didn't understand that to a lifelong grain farmer there could be nothing beautiful about a countryside that had lost its greenness from months without rain. In his practical soul he perceived, as I never had, that what we were looking at was, finally, farmland.

In the years when my wife and I were annual visitors, we were sitting one late afternoon in a very fine wine bar on the town square in Sonoma. Seated directly across from us, along the other leg of the bar's U, were a small cluster of men dressed in farmer's jeans and work shirts. Eavesdropping, it quickly became clear that they were vintners who had gathered at the end of a day in their vineyards. They were, in other words, indistinguishable in look and dress from the farmer who I as a boy, waiting to find the feel and idiom of the work, still imagined I might be: a young man sitting and trading gossip and crop talk over weak black coffee at the U-shaped counter of the Please-You Café on the town square in Prairie City.

These Sonoma vintners were, of course, drinking not weak black coffee but fine red wine. In fact, drinking a bit too much of it too quickly. For their conversation was boisterous, uninhibited, and shortly became a chorus of crude, blue complaint about the scant opportunities for the physical pleasures of romance in Sonoma, a town so small, with so little talent to choose from. Soon their language reached the point where I asked my wife if she wished me to speak to them, or to quickly finish our wine and leave.

It was just then that one in the group lifted his glass. As though this were a cue, everyone went still and they all paused to lift theirs, too, and then to expertly swirl and plunge their snouts in and take long assessing snorts. There was reverent meditation and then one of them murmured, "God damn, what a lovely nose."

"Got a 95 in the new *Wine Spectator*," said another.

"It deserves it," said a third.

"I'm getting licorice and, what? nutmeg? *Cinnamon*," said the first.

Crop talk.

Describing the challenge of making reds he could be proud of, Mason Groben spoke, as I mentioned, of the spring and summer rains that have historically broken a run of sunny days in the Midwest. But he went on to say that he struggled as much, maybe even more, with the soil's assertiveness. It's so relentlessly rich, he explained, so damned insistent, that left unchecked there'd be far too much of it bullying its way into the taste—the risk of what he calls a "foxy-ness, tasting like a pile of damp leaves."

The wine world talks, and rightly so, about the importance of *terroir* in defining a wine's character. But this assumes a soil that's been growing wine forever, a soil that has learned the intricate essence of its necessary role. But for what Mason Groben must contend with, it's as if the too-bold Iowa earth was trying to overwhelm his efforts at refinement, was determined to undermine this fancy new use to which it was being put. As if it were saying, *Terroir*? What we call it here is dirt.

It seemed clear to me that Mason Groben's abiding work at Jasper would be to find the balance: how much Iowa to let in and how much to keep out. My fantasies aside, this was what he and I had in common. How much Iowa to let in; how much Iowa to keep out. As a life and its conundrum, it's one I know about.

TOUCHING

⁓

IN THE YEARS I KNEW MY GRANDFATHER EVANS, HE BORE
no resemblance to the man I later learned of from my mother's
recollections—the profane coal miner, working the Midwest's
meager bituminous lode, whose nightly drinking started once
he'd finished scrubbing himself clean from his day beneath the
ground, and continued through supper and his remaining waking
hours, turning sullen or worse inside his nightly booze.

As a boy, I saw him almost every Sunday, when many of his
nine children and their families gathered to eat and spend the day.
By then he'd become a withdrawn invalid in his huge, shabby,
maroon-colored armchair, smelling of pipe tobacco and a kind of
lingering fungal rankness, sitting still as a squalid Buddha, listening on the radio in the summer to his beloved Chicago Cubs lose,
emitting a startling falsetto "Whooee!" when Dee Fondy or Gene
Baker or the great Ernie Banks hit a home run. But mostly, as I
said, sitting eerily quiet in his overalls and slippers in the corner
of his tiny living room next to the big coal stove, an ancient water
stain in the shape of South America on the wallpaper behind him.
I remember watching his fingertips press tobacco into the bowl
of his pipe, loose strands sprinkling the bib of his denim overalls,

his fingers ochre-stained from nicotine, his neglected nails long like a woman's and curled at their ends, creepy as claws. I conjure him sitting there, smoking, and staring out from beneath the bill of his accidentally dapper gray tweed driving cap through eyes that were dramatically whitened by cataracts.

I don't know why his cataracts were left to grow, though in his time—he was born in 1881—they were not routinely removed; the techniques and instruments were still relatively crude. And there was also the matter of his lifelong poverty. The answer, then, might be as simple as his having had neither the money nor the health.

For he suffered from other disabilities as well, including what I assume was a relatively contained case of black lung. His coughs, when they came, were fits of high inhuman sound that took possession of him and shook him in his chair. When he did leave that chair, with a struggle, in stages, he walked with wooden crutches, which creaked to my ears like a horror movie sound effect with each slow step.

But it was most of all his blindness that mesmerized and spooked me. The impression his whitened eyeballs made changed with the mood of my imagination. Sometimes I thought of them as scrims of tiny clouds; other times his cataracts looked hard as shells of porcelain.

As adults, we are disgusted and threatened by deformity. But when we're children, we're better than that. There's infatuation in our fear and our disgust is something sensual. We want goblins and witches in our worlds; they take our days and our dreams to a place beyond the ordinary, where days and dreams belong, and no witch, no goblin worth his salt, is not deformed or frightening. So if I didn't have a grandson's easy physical love for my grandfather, there was something in my feelings more compelling than that: in all his Grimms' vividness, he deliciously repulsed me.

But the charm of the goblin does not survive our childhoods. Or in fairness, I should say only that it did not survive mine. I think of my reaction when I was told that I myself had cataracts, of how that news sent a signal of grotesquerie and age. Or I think of when, volunteering in a homeless shelter, I initially recoiled at the condition and the reek of the men's gnarled feet as they lowered them to soak in the plastic basins of warm, soapy water I placed in front of them.

When I was a small boy, my first duty on arriving at my grandparents' for our regular Sunday visits and the big family dinner was to report to my grandfather for what he called "exercises." I assume all or most of my many cousins also had to endure this ritual, but I'm the only sufferer I remember. So before I could go outside to join the play, I stood before him in his shabby armchair and announced myself. He greeted me, smiling, and motioned me up onto his lap. I complied with great reluctance, facing him with my short legs straddling him. I felt his long, nicotine-stained fingers wrap themselves around mine.

And then our "exercises" began as he quickly lifted and lowered my arms, crossed them and extended them wide, drew them back and pulled them to his chest, repeating the sequence again and again, all the while keeping a strict, brisk beat with a lilting "Whee! Whee! Whee! Whee!" a variation on "Whooee!" and, like it, a sound of prepubescent joy.

In the midst of all this, I would look away to the several holes in the arms of his chair, most of them made from embers falling unnoticed from his pipe, which set the stuffing smoldering until he smelled the smoke and called for someone to bring a cup of dousing water. I remember a recurring dream, born of what I vaguely imagined about his days in the mines, of falling Alice-like through one of the armchair holes into a magical world where the air was visible and blue, like a sea become a sky, so thick and heavy I could barely breathe it. There were tables of tiny men eating and laughing, and there were animals of a kind I'd never seen, like friendly griffins, and the men and the animals spoke a language of melodious vowels. Always, in the dream, my lungs were just beginning to clear and I was about to understand some of the words when there was suddenly the threat of an overhead collapse, the men running around shouting and the animals frantic, and at that moment I woke.

"Whee! Whee! Whee! Whee!"

As much as I dreaded the thought of the exercises, once we started them I gradually gave over to their jostling meter and my discomfort with his touch and his tang began to fade. I sensed his strangeness softening, felt him briefly, recognizably *alive*. This odd regimen was the way I felt him feeling.

When we finished, I climbed down from his lap, almost dizzy, momentarily disoriented, and thanked him as I'd been instructed to do. He retreated then, back into his chrysalis of frailty. You could almost see and sense it happening—his alertness to the world leaving his face, in the way a drunk disappears into his drunkenness.

Once I'd outgrown the exercises, become too old and too big to sit on his lap, there was no particular reason to offer him my hands, to feel his touch, to endure the sensation of his fingers slowly wrapping themselves around my wrists. And so, unless I had to, a handshake he asked for now and then, I no longer touched my grandfather.

Remembering those Sundays at my grandparents' house, I see my mother moving back and forth in the kitchen, she and her sister helping their mother, who, despite her own infirmities, unfortunately insisted on continuing to cook the dinner. She was reputed to have been a wonderful cook, but at this point her roast beef was most often vulcanized, her mashed potatoes likely clods, grease almost certainly floating like oil slicks in her gravy. Luckily, she never lost her touch with the crusts of her fruit pies.

My grandmother was an uncomplaining woman, though her heavy-lidded eyes, mournful as a basset's, suggested she was expecting life's next great trial to arrive at any moment. In her body she was the victim of both her hard life and her genes. To the first she could attribute, among other things, her few remaining teeth sitting crookedly in her mouth, prominent as fangs; and to the second the fact that she was shaped remarkably like a pear. It was as though her flesh had long ago begun to slide until nearly all of it had settled well below her waist. Her calves were elephantine; the flesh of her ankles spilled out over the tops of the black, shapeless slippers she always wore.

But in contrast to my grandfather, she came *toward* me, *met* me, greeting me with hugs and delighted caws of welcome. It didn't matter that she had six teeth in her mouth and her body was a gargoyle's. And in response to the love she showed me, I felt real love for her; an unhesitant, uncomplicated love.

As I said, it was from my mother that I learned of my grandfather's drunken meanness. She obliquely sketched the picture in bits of memory over the years, though she never spoke of any physical violence, just his snarl, like a hostile animal, if you tried to engage him when he was drinking.

But her recollecting tone was never bitter or residually fearful; in my memory it sounded a kind of complicated nostalgia.

She often visited the house in Colfax on days that weren't Sunday in order to assist with a task or run an errand. On the day I'm recalling—I was maybe ten or eleven—I went with her. Returning from the nearby playground, I opened the door, stepped into the kitchen, and aimlessly turned toward the living room. From there, it was possible to look to the right and see at an angle into my grandparents' bedroom, doorway giving to doorway and then the framed partial view, like an intimate Vermeer warren.

Movement from the bedroom drew my eye and I looked through to see my mother and grandmother standing face to face beside the bed. My mother's back was to me; neither of them sensed me.

My grandmother's dress was bunched at her neck like a great

collapsed ruffle. Her slip was off her shoulders and draped from her waist. The corpse-whiteness of her skin was a color no palette could capture. But what shocked me were the ghoulish append-ages that were her breasts—wide, flat straps of flesh that hung below her waist and ended bulbously.

My mother was saying something to her, too softly for me to get her words, while she lifted a washcloth from a pan of soapy water sitting on the bed, wrung it out, and continued to wash her mother's body. My grandmother stood, patiently receiving my mother's care, their murmurs so casual they might have been trading bits of homely gossip as they knitted side by side. My grandmother was certainly able to wash herself, so I've no idea why this was happening.

I turned away, shocked and disgusted. There was no goblin charm in *this* glimpse of deformity. It was far too vivid, far too actual. But stunned as I was, what has stayed with me is the picture of my mother's ministering ease. It was as though, like a conscientious tradesman, she was applying with careful brush strokes a more expert cleanliness than my grandmother could have achieved on her own. In their postures and composure they *were* Vermeer figures absorbed in the amber domesticity of un-remarkable chores.

My grandfather was the first dead person I saw. I was nearly thir-teen and, as I remember, my being readied for what to expect at his funeral consisted of my mother warning me that "Grandpa won't look like himself" as he lay in his open casket. I don't re-member if she tried to describe what he'd look like instead.

The service was held in the funeral home's chapel, a small, windowless room with forest-green walls. I sat between my par-ents in the front row of folding chairs. Family flanked us and filled rows behind us. My grandmother was not with us. Her heft and her arthritis had by now made it impossible for her to fit into a car or climb a set of steps. My Aunt Mable had stayed behind to be with her. The rest of us had filed past her in her chair as we left the house, bending down to kiss her cheek or touching her shoulder or her arm or patting her hand in which she held a balled-up white embroidered handkerchief that was wet with her tears.

The minister stood at a small podium, an organ and organist to his right, my grandfather in a casket to his left.

My mother had been right: he did not look like himself. What he looked like instead was remarkably neat and clean. He'd been transformed, not so much by death as by hygiene. His thin white hair was parted and combed. His death-complexion face was whiskerless and rouged. He wore a suit and tie, surely purchased for this ultimate appearance. I'd never seen him in anything but bib overalls. He was surrounded, not by ratty, burn-holed maroon cloth but by shiny cream-colored satin. I picture his body in profile in a cone of light. This is doubtless what my memory has incorrectly fashioned. If he'd mesmerized me as a blind old ghoul on crutches, the thrilling strangeness of his corpse was greater than anything I could have dreamt or imagined. Stranger than tiny men below the earth who breathed the sea-blue air and spoke in vowels.

I couldn't keep from looking at him.

But glancing around, I saw everyone else's eyes fixed on the minister, who also did not turn or nod in my grandfather's direction as he recited the dates and facts of his life. It was as if his body was pointless to acknowledge now that his soul had risen, now that death had rid it of the stored lifetime of thoughts and feelings and left it no more relevant than a husk. Either that or the opposite—as if his corpse, all mystery and material, spirit and shape, was too overwhelmingly *present* to look at.

But he seemed to me too present *not* to. Also, death's stillness gave him a kind of poised dignity he'd only in death been able to achieve. And maybe because I'd watched him so often sitting as quiet and motionless in life as he lay now, I imagined him suddenly reverting to undignified form and popping up in his coffin to sound a "Whooee!"

And then I realized my mother was weeping. How long she had been, I didn't know. Her shoulders were moving subtly, and she was patting her eyes with a tissue. At last here was something that made sense: a father was dead and his daughter was sad.

Or did and did *not* make sense, for I was surprised to see her weeping. As I understood emotions and what they signaled, her weeping was evidence that she held deep feelings for him. These were feelings I hadn't imagined she had. A sense of duty, yes; devotion, yes; but nothing like what I thought she was conveying now. I'd seen her over the years show him a kind of steady custodial attention, seen her bending to him to ask him how he felt and if he needed anything. I'd seen her tidying up around his chair, picking up wrappers and papers he'd unknowingly dropped in his lap or on the floor. I'd seen her cutting his food into the small bites he preferred so he could eat with a spoon. I'd seen her attending to him, but I had no memory of her *tending* to him. Of her touching him in any way that wasn't brief and requisite. In my child's simplistic sense of things, this meant I'd never seen her make a gesture of love toward her father.

It had been some years since I'd sat in his lap and offered him my hands and felt his fingers with their long, neglected nails wrap serpentinely around my wrists and sensed him come to sweetly silly life. I'd forgotten how it felt to feel him feeling.

As a grandson I hadn't loved him simply, viscerally, instinctively, and I'd assumed without thinking that these were the ways my mother also hadn't loved him. Sitting next to her, I was surprised, I was confused, to see, as I interpreted her weeping, that she'd loved him to the depth that the act of weeping proved. Loved the old man whose ailments cocooned him from life; loved the earlier man who cocooned himself from it when he drank.

I started a soft, ragged breathing in time with hers, while my upper body slightly trembled to show her how much sorrow I was working to hold in. And in pretending sadness so strenuously I beckoned it. I felt a small, clean moment of sadness come. After some seconds, my mother leaned closer to me. She reached for my hand and until she'd covered it with hers I didn't know you could feel comforted and fraudulent, both at once.

Clearing her apartment after her death, I discovered in her bedroom bureau drawers—among the dozens of albums and envelopes loosely stuffed with photos, the dish of souvenir bills and coins, the letters and seasonal cards—among all of that I found something she'd written and kept for more than seventy years. It was a story, a fable she composed, quite lovely prose filling three lined sheets of notebook paper and signed "Maude Evans, Age 13." If it was a school assignment, the pages bear no marks or comments from a teacher, and no grade. Perhaps it was something she wrote in Sunday school, for the fable's narrator is the family Bible, speaking from its place on the library shelves. Formally, then, experimental fiction, a tale from the point of view of a book—indeed, the *Book*.

"A rather strict but happy home, this family . . . ," the Bible-narrator begins fragmentedly.

"The mother is a sweet and lovable person. . . . The father was a rather prompt and decisive man but very kind to his children, seeming to be a small boy again when one of the boys told him the happenings of the day.

"The youngest daughter was worshipped by all the family. A rather pale and delicate child and like her brother John, loved nature."

The story describes a winter blizzard, an event the family—being wise and orderly—prepared for by feeding the livestock early and stacking extra firewood. The snowstorm kept them housebound for two nights, during which they all "enjoyed themselves by reading books, including myself, and telling stories." The third morning the sun shone and "teamsters came to break away the snow drifts from the road."

And since then, "Time has passed . . . and now only two faithful members remain in the home, John and his brother." As well as the narrator, still sitting "on the library shelf, to have my pages turned."

I needn't belabor the parallels and, so, the differences between my mother's childhood and the one she invented. Her brooding, unapproachable father in his cups compared to the story's prompt, kind father, so empathic he became a boy again when his boys described their days to him. My mother's family, one of her sisters dead at birth, another at thirty, leaving orphaned children, her parents failing prematurely; that family versus one of implicitly healthy, clean-living nature lovers. My mother's childhood in a family on the bare margin, nine children raised on a coal miner's wages; and a fictional life with many fewer children and ample stores of firewood and shelves filled with books, in a household where you can virtually smell the bleached, starched spotlessness of things. And finally, my mother, the youngest daughter, doubtless loved, but living among often roistering brothers, one of whom once threw a clawing cat in her face; and the story's youngest daughter, worshipped, pale and delicate.

Pale and delicate was not an option for my mother.

I wonder still, as I wondered that day, what she was grieving at her father's funeral. The childhood she'd lived, or the one that had eluded her—a fantasy as far from reality as a dream of falling through a burn hole in a chair into a world of sea-blue air? Was she mourning the father she lost, or the one she never had? Was she weeping for a kindness recalled, or a cruelty remembered? For some warmth or wit I didn't know he'd once possessed, or for being reminded by his death that he'd never possessed it?

I wonder what he'd done for her—done once, or frequently, or habitually—that had touched her?

But there's a crucial difference, now from then. I still can't know what she was weeping for, but looking back I'm not surprised that she was weeping. Sitting next to her, wanting to catch up to her sadness in the hope of understanding it, I was years from having any sense at all of the intricate texture of love for a parent. Which is to say, I was years from understanding love of any kind, for anyone—that inseparable braiding of gratitude and hurt; of what we get and don't get; of the simplicity of what we're sure we'll feel forever and the grand complexity of all we come to feel besides.

I remember now another reason for touching my grandfather, or for letting him touch me. If, as family lore had it, you wanted to be rid of some unpleasant or bothersome blemish, some wart or mole or pimple, he would "buy it from you." He gave you a penny, then touched whatever it was you wished removed, holding the tip of his index finger on it for some moments, and after a while, say a month, it went away. As I remember, he didn't acquire the blemish himself. Perhaps that's what the payment of the penny guaranteed.

Everyone in the family, all my aunts and uncles, and most importantly, my mother, swore that he possessed this power.

Is this a long buried childhood dream I once had about my grandfather? Is it, like the world of tiny men, something I once fantasized? Whatever its source, I have a memory of him working his magic successfully on me, asking me to take his hand and guide it to a wart growing in the corner of the cuticle on my left thumb.

And does my mother's supporting testimony suggest that, as a girl, she and her siblings decided to give him this power, making him much more than a bad-tempered drunk, but also a father who could take away your imperfections with his sorcerer's touch? Is that who she was weeping for?

I sometimes imagined the map lines of my mother's many surgical scars, from the oldest and only faintly visible to those more recent and prominent—some perhaps overlapping, some roughly paralleling one another. In her long life of setbacks and dogged recoveries, she had her thyroid gland removed; she had an operation to remove a rib; she had quadruple bypass surgery; she had a cancerous tumor removed from her cheek; she had an artificial hip implanted to replace the one she broke after falling in her kitchen.

The only scars from all these surgeries I saw were the first, resulting from the removal of her thyroid—long faded but which she often hid with a scarf or a necklace—and the last, the vertical incision along her left hip, which ran as neatly as though drawn with the help of a ruler, and which had quieted considerably, with little redness, less than two weeks after the replacement surgery.

The last summer of her life, five months before she died, I sat in her apartment with her and an aide from the hospital rehabilitation staff. I'd come from Boston, relieving my brother, who'd stayed with her for a week and arranged for her postsurgical care.

The aide was a woman in her late thirties, early forties, broadfaced, her hair styled in a way I'd describe as incoherent—coils of it hanging loosely like sprung springs. She exuded the Midwest's big, plain, loudly broadcast friendliness, and she'd come to look at my mother's apartment to determine what it would need to help ease her recuperation. Where grab bars and handles should be installed, which shelves should be lowered, which chairs were too low, which throw rugs were hazardous.

Early in the conversation, the woman looked up from her notes and asked my mother whether it was her left or right hip that had been replaced.

"The left," my mother said.

"May I see?" the woman asked.

I was sitting in an armchair between them and I looked nervously from her to my mother. For some reason I heard, in the easeful manner of the caretaker's purely professional request, a hint of prurience. I don't know why, I was certainly wrong, and I've decided my reaction had to do with what the question touched in me.

Maybe it touched the same thing in my mother. For I thought I saw just an instant of alarm in her face at the question and I imagined her thinking, *With my son sitting here between us?* Which would have been her version of just what I was thinking—*With me sitting here between you, not ten feet away?*

But she dutifully scooted forward on her couch as the woman stood and passed in front of me. She bent down to look, her loose coils of hair swinging forward, as my mother raised the hem of her robe just high enough.

What were the rules here? Had I been asked, with the aide's question, to take a look as well? A clinical inspection that might be of practical help to me? Or should I, according to some sort of decorum— and fearing whatever I feared I might see—look away? Wanting not to look, or rather wanting not to see, I furtively glimpsed the brief, trig cut traveling my mother's busy-veined white thigh.

"That's healing great," the aide said.

"I haven't really felt a lot of pain," my mother said. "Even right after."

And that was all, the instant passed, quick and antiseptic and unrevealing, and I felt a moment of enormous relief that some first episode of awful intimacy had been postponed.

I picture the clinical gentleness with which my mother washed her mother's body. How would it have been if I were called upon to help my mother bathe, to help her dress and undress, or to help her in those moments of final infant weakness? I'll never know, for such a moment never came, when I took her arm to help her keep her balance as she stood next to me beside her bathtub, her free hand slowly working its way down a row of big buttons on her quilted robe. As I then helped her out of the robe and held her gently but steadily—where? by her shoulders? at her waist?—and, naked now, her scars like body art, a network of necessary violence, she managed with excruciating slowness to step over the lip of the narrow tub. And as I then placed my hands under her arms to lower her into the heated water, her hair below flesh folds a patch of wet gray moss, to assist her with a kind of impervious kindness.

In the way—it occurs to me—that it got to be routine to guide a homeless man's ruined feet into a tub of soothing water.

But no, that only tells me how easy it became to touch the scars and aged flesh of a stranger.

THE LIFE HE LEFT HER

༃

MY FATHER DIED SEVEN YEARS BEFORE MY MOTHER WOULD, and some months after his death, while visiting her, I walked from her apartment to the village cemetery, a distance of two blocks, to look at the gray marble gravestone. It had just recently been set. Reaching it, I saw that its polished face was relatively plain: just their names, and touches of scrollwork in the upper corners, but none of the beveled filigree distinguishing many of the neighboring stones.

When I returned to her apartment, she was waiting eagerly for my opinion. Did I think the stone looked too bare? I said no, that its simplicity was elegant, which was true. But I could tell my words did little to reassure her. She said she wished she'd ordered a marble base. She was worried that the stone's sitting directly on the ground made it appear unfinished, incomplete.

She seemed to be fretting that the baseless stone and its design might reflect poorly on her taste and, I thought, even more on her generosity. I imagined her worrying that, in the judgment of her self-scrutinizing little town, the stone's spareness only showed that she'd scrimped on the cost. In other words, not thinking it through, I regarded the stone that first day I saw it as marking my father's life and its end, not ultimately hers too, and certainly not their life together. She was, after all, still quite vibrantly alive. Which partly, but only partly, explains why I felt this way. And why I assumed it was how she thought of the stone, too.

In my parents' nearly sixty years of marriage, there were no public treacheries, no flagrant adulteries. Instead, their years together as I saw them comprised a long narrative of quiet erosion, colored chiefly by the steady wearing away of her respect for him. And in reaction, his retreat into a silent obduracy.

My mother was an almost comically ardent Midwest chauvinist. She bristled whenever she heard some East Coast wag on radio or television make a crack about a hick farmer from Iowa. It was a label she both resented and was burdened by, cringing whenever she encountered what she saw as confirming evidence that it fit. I remember her once standing in the kitchen at the ironing board, shaking her head at the radio and muttering, disgusted, "Oh, good lord," as she listened to an interview with one of the state's long-serving senators, a man with the perfectly Dickensian name of Bourke B. Hickenlooper. The hard-consonant whine of his voice as she heard it sent visions of milking stalls and hog lots out into the world.

I believe she lived in a kind of mortal terror of my father doing something that would reveal him to be a hick farmer from Iowa and her, the wife of one. Once, in Boston, they took Sue and me to brunch, and at the end of the meal my father got the check and put down his credit card. But he'd not tucked the card into the leatherette folder's little plastic pocket so the waiter could see it. Noting this, my mother made a sound of complete exasperation, a prosecutorial near-syllable, moist and mean, at the back of her throat. Then she opened the folder and, rolling her eyes, put the credit card into the plastic pocket.

Imagine the effect of such relentless monitoring, of his knowing she was waiting for his next mistake as he chose the wrong spot in a parking lot, arranged suitcases in the trunk in the wrong order, chose the wrong shirt to wear, the wrong living-room lamp to turn on. And the result in him was a kind of silent-film sped-up jumpiness as he offered the wrong hand or rushed to open the wrong door.

Earlier in their marriage, when I was growing up, I recall that she got angriest when she accused my father of drinking too much, of being drunk. I remember the scene, reenacted countless times, of her meeting him at the door when he got home from the village later than she thought he should have. *Where have you been? . . . Don't lie to me . . . I can smell it on your breath.*

I remember sitting in the back seat of the car coming home from various occasions over the years, their two heads up front like flanking busts in darkness. *You're drunk . . . Pull over . . . Do you want to kill us all?*

Why this particular accusation, I can't know. In the years when they were dating, and as a young married couple when my father was a soldier in the Second World War, lots of social drinking had simply been part of the play. But now, in fact and in her mind, she was very far from that world of smiling antics. Could it be that she missed it even more keenly than I've imagined, and any vestige of it, any sense that my father continued to enjoy it by having some beers with some buddies at the only tavern in the village, enraged her? If that spirit was gone from her life, it had damn well better be gone from his?

I must also keep in mind that, as a girl and young woman, she lived in an unruly house where her father was a drunk, and a mean one. And I wonder, now that her life was so severely domestic, if some of her vigilance came from the memory of how it had been to live with him. I know that memories of childhood are notoriously unreliable, but I believe my mother's, of her growing up, were not. She was not merely remembering episodes that might have happened in her house. She was remembering its persistent nightly climate.

As for me and the memories of *my* childhood, I don't recall my father ever being drunk in my presence.

As clearly as I hear the particular pitch of her anger when they argued, I don't remember, cannot hear, my father's voice at all. And when I try to imagine the words they might have traded out of earshot, about anything—about my grandparents staying in the farmhouse too long; about my father's acceptance, even welcoming their staying; or his denying he was late coming home from town; denying he was drunk and driving us home—I can again easily hear her voice, fiercely charged, but not the sound of his and not the words of his response.

But if, over time, he came to be cowed by her and a man who reflexively submitted to the preferences of others, he also developed with his deference an enormous stubbornness running beneath it. Often his way of getting what he wanted in the end was simply not to do what he'd said he would when it went against some stronger, private wish.

In his last decade, their talk became increasingly about the need to sell the farmhouse. He had fallen and broken his hip, as she would, and though his recovery was in the strictest sense complete, it left him living with some pain. He had already begun to feel the house was too much to maintain, and after his fall it grew to be a burden he could not deny. But he'd lived nearly all his life in rambling farmhouses, in country solitude, and when you've been accustomed for so long to so much room in your world, where could you find a place to live that didn't feel like a motel room?

And so, in the matter of his agreeing they must sell the house, his stronger, private wish was not to live anywhere else. Having made the hard decision, and despite her formidable prodding, he proceeded to do nothing about it. But once the word got out there were eager buyers anyway, particularly a young couple whose desire for the place was so keen that they contractually agreed to wait to take possession until Mom and Dad had decided where to move.

In the following months, while the new owners waited, my parents talked and talked inconclusively about where they might go. During this time his pain became stronger and steadier and more and more he lost his appetite. As he grew increasingly uncomfortable and unhappy, he spoke of there being such a thing as living too long and that his body was proof of it. Puttering one day in the garage where he kept his tools, he somehow slipped and fell a second time, as again my mother would, and broke his other hip, as she would not, and once in the hospital he this time seized the invitation of his accident and his bed. It took him ten days. He'd turned eighty-three a week before he died and in dying managed to solve the insoluble contradiction. He'd sold his house and also met his stronger, private wish not to live anywhere else.

The day after his funeral, I went with my mother to their bank to get a life insurance policy from their safe-deposit box so that she could start the process of redeeming it. The bank manager, her gray hair cut in a Louise Brooks bob, offered her condolences as she led us into the room where the boxes were kept. She was the same woman who, seven years later, would offer me a disapproving look when, intending admiration, I called my mother "mean."

At first we took the time to pause and reflect on the various items as we removed them from the box. We found several contracts tracing the ownership of the farm, one a handwritten abstract from 1890, its perfect, ornate cursive a beautiful calligraphy. If I asked a question about some document and she knew the answer, she let her memory take as long as it wished in her reply as gradually the papers started to pile up on the table.

I had no idea how much the insurance policy was worth. I knew it would hardly make her wealthy. But it was clear to her, remembering his assurances that she needn't worry when he was gone, that combined with Social Security, it would greatly help to ease her deep and understandable anxieties about money. She'd be able to live in an apartment of reasonable size, maintain the 1998 bottle-green Buick, and go with a friend after church for Sunday dinner at her favorite franchise restaurant, all without having to ask herself whether she could afford it.

At the bank, in the safe-deposit box room, we'd yet to come upon the policy, and our working rhythm increasingly became one of alert cooperation. Reach in, withdraw, quickly examine and discard, her turn, my turn, her turn, my turn. As more and more documents accumulated the nostalgia began to leave her voice, our task now resembling some mindless children's game—Crazy Eights or Pick-up Sticks—that requires no skill and involves no strategy. There was no skill or strategy in our game either, just a mounting need for one of us, either of us, to win.

At last I spotted the policy. "Ah, here it is." I handed it to her as though presenting a much overdue award.

She looked at it, with its tissue-thin pages in a light-blue cover, and immediately said, "That's not it." She put it down and when I picked it up to look again I saw that it was a policy she'd taken out herself, for two thousand dollars, naming my brother as the beneficiary.

We returned our attention to the safe-deposit box.

We withdrew several contracts from the 1930s on, documenting the shrewd commercial maneuverings of my Grandfather Bauer. Ten acres acquired here, six acres sold there. I felt my worry building, building. Could my mother be wrong? Had she misunderstood? I simply couldn't believe where this moment seemed to be going.

We found my father's honorable discharge from the Army on the fifth of February, 1946, ending his military career as a dental technician at Fort Francis E. Warren in Cheyenne, Wyoming.

We found a copy of my Wyoming birth certificate, which was for some reason boldly stamped "unverified." I thought to make a joke and then, in the midst of the mood, thought again.

We found two copies of their certificate of marriage, witnessed, naturally, by their parents. I couldn't picture Grandmother or Grandfather Evans, both so infirm in the years I knew them, being ambulatory enough to attend a ceremony, even their daughter's wedding, on June 5, 1942, less than a decade before they were the invalids I knew.

These documents, like much else we came upon, had histories I'd have normally wanted to hear and she'd have wanted to tell me about. Glancing at her, I saw her eyes squinting with every piece of paper she reached for. We said nothing more and through the diction of our silence her face was growing increasingly pinched, looking as if she were trying to draw a badly frayed thread through a needle's eye.

Until we'd finished emptying the box.

We subsided into our high-backed chairs, into a silence made by the room and by our dumb shock, life in all its wrenching artlessness, as she sat with the revelation that what she'd understood to be true about essential things was not.

I fought the urge to lean forward again and peer down into the box; to turn it upside down and shake it.

I've tried many times to imagine her feelings as she sat there. But the best I can do is an image of an immediate eclipse, darkness drawing swiftly across the terrain of what she'd thought her coming years would be.

We sat for what was probably not very long. My mind was frantic with questions. Had she ever actually seen a policy, or had he simply said there was one when there wasn't? Was there a chance it had been taken from the safe-deposit box? Maybe packed with other papers when she'd moved from the farm? Was it possible he'd actually cashed it? And was that even legally permissible without the presence and signature of its beneficiary? If it wasn't, this meant he had to have invented the whole thing, safe in his assurance that she'd never ask to see it. But for God's sake, why? Yes, I'd known him as a man who prevailed by quietly not doing what he said he would; but not as one who secretly hadn't done what he said he had.

I had no idea what to offer her, whether consolation, indignation, or disbelief. Any and all of these seemed appropriate, and not remotely enough. She appeared stunned, naturally, but when at last she spoke her voice was calm, her tone conclusive.

"It's my own fault. When it came to the money, I just let him handle it. I should have kept track of what was going on, but I didn't. I never paid attention." She shook her head and repeated, "It's my own fault."

It was as if she'd already answered for herself every question that had come to me, and others that had not. The only one left for her was not if or how but when he'd cashed it in. She'd been sitting there, the very air suffused with her heart's humiliation, silently summoning and reviewing, I suppose, various times in their life together when it looked as if money was going to be scarce, and then it had turned out that everything was fine.

The idea of her being inattentive was, to say the least, hard for me to fathom. I couldn't imagine her as anything other than fiercely overseeing any task he performed and it surely speaks to the inflexible mores of their generation, or at least to the way she understood them, that for better or worse, in sickness and in health, money was the husband's province.

"I'm really sorry, Mom. I'm . . . really sorry."

Lines in her face converged at her puckered mouth like tightened netting. But even as she fought tears, she continued to give off that particular calm when the terms of a grief are recognized.

We sat a minute longer until she'd composed herself, then she gathered up some papers and we put everything else back in the box and she locked it again.

In the lobby, as she was handing back the key, one of the tellers came around from behind the long counter and took her hand. "I'm so sorry," she said. "He was such a great guy. It was always fun when he came in. He was so friendly, so easy to talk to."

My mother brought a grim genius to moments such as this. No one I've known received the bitter, ironic comedy of life more readily, perhaps because it so confirmed her view of it. She managed a weak smile that the teller doubtless saw as sorrowful affection. "It's true," she said, "he could talk to anyone. When we went to the mall in Des Moines, he'd wait for me on a bench outside a store and I'd come out and he'd be having a great conversation with some total stranger."

"We'll miss him so," said the teller.

We stepped outside and met the August day's sodden heat. After the awful exchange with the unwitting teller, I felt a need to fill the even more freighted silence and offered stupidly, "You know, Mom, there are two sides to all of us. The way we are in private and the way we are in the world. And they're both real. I mean, what I'm saying, his public self, the friendly guy who could start a conversation with anyone, that's genuinely who he was, too."

She'd been nodding regularly as I spoke, as if my nonsense had a meter. "Yes," she said, "they were both in him, those qualities. They're in all of us. The trouble was, with Dad . . . they were too far apart."

During the week I spent cleaning out her apartment after she died, I worked one afternoon to empty her bedroom. As the winter day darkened, I turned on the bedside lamp and opened a bureau drawer to find scrapbooks and photo albums and envelopes stuffed with snapshots. I sat down on the floor and spread them out before me. There was a powerful fascination in seeing people I'd known so well for so long—my many aunts and uncles; my parents' friends—growing older or younger, depending on the order in which I picked up the photos: becoming steadily heavier or increasingly gaunt, balder, flesh looser, faces more lined. But what really made me linger were the dozens of pictures of my parents from the years my father was a soldier in Cheyenne, Wyoming.

They were newlyweds when she joined him there. And for nearly four years, till the end of the war, they lived what I believe was far and away their happiest time. Their achingly young faces in these snapshots were the faces I'd pictured when I heard them recalling those years. There was one of them with their arms around each other, my father's lips pursed as if ready to whistle wolfishly. On the back of the photo, as if captioning a cartoon, she'd written, "What were you doing whistlin' Kenny?" Another, the same pose, my father as always in uniform, bore her written comment to whomever she sent it, "Lousy of me, but pretty cute of my hubbie, don't you think?" and I read in that endearment, "hubbie," a young and sweetly eager claim. There was a photo of her poised to throw a snowball toward the camera, and her smile this time was mischievously charming. "April snowstorm in Cheyenne!!" she'd written on the back. There are several of her and a couple of my father holding me, the clueless fat-cheeked newborn, my tiny body all askew in their arms.

The breadth of pleasure, and all its nuances, that the photos capture convey a disposition I never saw in their faces or heard in their voices when I was old enough to note that, except for the occasional Cheyenne recollection, it wasn't there.

But again and again, in photo after photo, their smiles suggested that life's pleasures could be sometimes bold and sometimes subtle, sometimes plain and sometimes intricate, and always buoyantly close to illicit. Whatever they thought they were and imagined they might become, they knew—and especially, I'm sure, my mother knew—that they were not hick farmers from Iowa. And, for all that she could tell, they would never be.

Many times since the day I sat with my mother in the bank I've been tempted to see the missing life insurance policy as melodrama—my father's revenge from the grave. But that makes his mind Machiavellian, and it wasn't. To the extent he got revenge, it was accidental. He was a man who lived in dread of her caustic disapproval—that part of him was real as well; that was who he was, too—and I believe some particularly desperate wish to elude it wouldn't let him tell her what he'd done that had brought the need for money. Or what he'd done to get it. Which leaves the unanswerable questions of exactly what he did. And how heavily he suffered in living with it. And for how long.

Among all these questions, the only one I know the answer to, thanks to the lawyer who helped me settle my mother's estate, is that the purchaser of a life insurance policy is its owner, and has the right to cash it in without the knowledge of its beneficiary.

But here's the thing: in the last few years of my mother's life, something like that buoying Cheyenne lightness came into her voice when she spoke of him. Her tone grew warm. Her descriptions were fond. His foibles were recast, becoming ingrained quirks and not the behavior that had maddened her for decades. His recalcitrance became the constitutional resolve of a "stubborn German." This was a description she seemed weirdly prideful in awarding him, and she did so frequently, in a tone of begrudging affection. (Believe me when I say that, other than the surname, there was nothing about my father or his father or the culture of their households that hinted remotely at the customs of a German heritage, except, perhaps, their fondness for sauerkraut.)

It was in general as if she were recalling a scampish renegade, shrugging her shoulders as if to say, *What was a gal to do?* Given what I'd witnessed of their years together, and what I knew of his betrayal, it was incredible to me that such genuine feeling could appear, or resume. I'm not speaking of memories, of her liking to recall the years when they were young, although she did that, too. Nor am I describing an old woman whose mind had become susceptible to confusion or nostalgia. Hers, to put it mildly, had not. It was the quality, the simplicity, of her regard for him—it was *this* that sounded young. Her voice had found that Cheyenne timbre. She seemed wholly untroubled when she invoked his name, except for her sadness that he was gone.

So I picture her in Cheyenne, with all her many varieties of smile, and again at the close of her life, talking of my father in a spirit of fresh infatuation. I see the span of her years and these paired emotions at the beginning and the end. At the start, her innocent excitement for the life they had and, she thought, would have. At the last, her grand alteration of the life they in fact had.

During the time I spent in her apartment, I sat the first morning at her kitchen table with the contents of her purse spread out before me. In her wallet there were various business cards from companies and agencies I needed to call. There were a few credit cards I needed to cancel. I picked up her checkbook and began to scan the register. It felt invasive to do so. It seemed an act of violation. For here, somehow more nakedly than anywhere else, was her life in her years alone revealed: what it had cost her to live it.

The checks to her landlord were by far the largest. The last she'd written in her life was to him, entered in her register, impeccably responsible as always, on January first, eight days before she fell on the ice. She'd also written much smaller ones to the telephone company and the drugstore and the grocery on the square. Then, with little variance—an occasional check to Wal-Mart for something or other, never much more than twenty dollars—she'd written these same few checks again.

With everything I'd known about how little money she had, it was this stark arithmetic of her expenses, their unwavering recurrence dated and recorded, which brought home to me the remarkably spare commerce of her last years.

Of course she'd scrimped on the cost of their gravestone. What choice had she had?

There were two other regular checks, these written weekly. One, "Hair," was to the local beauty parlor. It was usually for $12.84, though now and then she paid a few dollars more for something extra.

The other weekly check, recorded just below "Hair," and always for $12, was to the "Church." At first it was the amount that caught my interest. Twelve dollars a week; six hundred and twenty-four dollars a year. How had she arrived at that figure? I pictured her sitting down with the sums and long division of her life, compiling a list of its clear necessities and coming up with the figure she could afford to give each week without risking the embarrassment of a Sunday when she couldn't.

But as I thought about it, it was not the amount of the check but the weekly writing of it, regular as a healthy heartbeat, that impressed me. Seeing "Church" repeatedly entered in her shaky, once-perfect Palmer-method penmanship was like coming on a contract she'd signed and signed and signed. Every week she wrote God a check for as much as she could give Him. But for me it somehow also seemed to echo more broadly than that—seemed in general a statement of fidelity, alliance, of dogged conviction.

Sometimes, thinking about their marriage, I've remembered Willa Cather's great novella, *My Mortal Enemy*, where Myra Henshawe is filled with a bitter resentment that her long marriage has not continued the unsustainably romantic moment that began it. Dying, she's asked why she's treated her husband so severely, and she replies, "Perhaps I can't forgive him for the harm I did him."

Perhaps my mother forgave my father for the harm she did him. Perhaps, that is, she came to see that the person she was as a wife contributed vitally to his deceit. Which would mean, of course—and I very much hope this was true—that she was then able to forgive herself. A forgiveness full enough that she could sit down one day and open her checkbook to worry about money, which was surely *every* day, which was surely constantly, and not have its niggardly columns of additions and subtractions stir her resentment for what he'd done. And so she was perhaps also able, another day, to visit the gravestone and see it as finished, and tastefully simple, and theirs.

Still, she must have spent hours in her last years trying to imagine his actions. Picturing him, maybe, defeatedly shaking his head, having spun some tale of woe for the insurance agent, as he signed the necessary papers in his office. Envisioning him taking a check to the bank for its deposit. Hearing him charming the tellers, as always—*Such a great guy. We'll miss him so*—with his schmoozy small-town patois.

It seems to me that the only way she could have placed him convincingly in any of these scenes was to imagine him as someone else, not my withdrawn father whose domestic bumbling was only made worse by his awareness that she watching through her unforgiving lens. Unconsciously, not delusionally, over time, she might have explained his great deception to herself by letting a kind of hybrid emerge—the handsome young rapscallion of the snapshots in Cheyenne with his ate-the-canary grin and his mischievously puckering lips about to whistle, but turned devious and scheming. To do what he did, and yet receive her valedictory adoration, he would have needed to possess a boldly devious impulse. He would have needed to be a guileful version of the man she loved as a newlywed. That man, that rascal, that stubborn German, would possess the lawless spirit willing to lie to save his ass.

So she forgot or ignored or forgave his betrayal, and maybe her final feelings for him should be seen not as distorted but reconciled, even wise in the beneficence they apparently achieved. Or as her determination not to be a victim to be pitied. Or as her need to justify their marriage to herself, which let her take them all the way back to Cheyenne. In the end, at the end, that's where she wanted them to be. And who am I to say it wasn't just the place for them?

Two days after she died I drove with my brother to that same bank to visit that same hermetic room to open that same safe-deposit box to fetch my parents' wills. Opening the box, we spotted them quickly, folded faux-parchment in stiff white envelopes lettered in Olde English. Each document is brief and straightforward, only two pages long. The language is identically plain, saying simply that, because all they had was jointly owned, whoever survived the other would inherit everything.

HOSS'S KNEE

ॐ

"WHEN I SAW THESE I THOUGHT, 'HOW IS THIS MAN WALKING?'"
This was Dr. Matzkin's way of introducing herself, holding up
my X-rays as she entered the exam room. There was a kind of
collegial jauntiness in her tone that made me think for a moment
she was about to show me someone else's: *You think your knee's
bad. Take a look at this guy's.* In any case, it was certainly a greeting
that gets a person's attention, and after shaking hands she showed
me why she'd said what she said.

I saw my left knee in the X-ray as a ghostly, shadow-white
sculpture coming almost three-dimensionally out of the black
background. I saw the mirroring curvature of its construction,
the long bones subtly parenthesizing the kneecap. It's an aes-
thetically lovely hinge, the knee: part Giacometti, part playful
Calder mobile. But what impressed me about mine, more than
the gracefulness and wit of its design, was the way the femur sat
absolutely squarely atop the tibia on the inner half of my knee.

More than forty years ago, in that prehistoric time before
minimally invasive arthroscopy, the surgeon made a long diago-
nal incision, crossing from inner knee to outer just below the
kneecap, in order to extract the ripped-up cartilage, the medial

meniscus. Through the years, I'd gotten used to hearing and feeling bits of loose calcium moving around, like gravel crunching and sifting, in the joint. I'd imagined tiny chips falling from the bones' increasingly jagged edges. I'd assumed these edges met like rows of broken teeth. But I was wrong. Without shock-absorbing cartilage between the two bones, they'd been rubbing against each other all that time, a relentless sanding, and they'd achieved a breathtaking smoothness, what appeared on the X-ray to be a perfectly horizontal hairline seam. Looking, I thought of the precisely fitting stones of Aztec pyramids.

Dr. Matzkin was also quite impressed. Not because such a definitive resting of bone on bone was unusual; she saw it frequently. But in her experience it meant prohibitive pain. Pain I'd been inexplicably lucky not to have. For years I'd been unable to fully flex the knee. But only recently had it begun to throb and stiffen if I took a long walk or stood for any length of time. When I got up after sitting for a while, the knee needed half a dozen steps to get loose.

I sat on Dr. Matzkin's examination table, my legs dangling from the edge, as she checked along my calf and my foot for a strong pulse. I'm happy to say she found one. She next compared the relative strength of my knees by placing her palm on my right shin and asking me to lift my lower leg against the pressure she was applying. She repeated the test with my left and, good Lord, I could barely lift it. I felt like a wimp, as if I'd lost some match of strength to a girl. I suspect this had to do in no small part with the fact that Dr. Matzkin is an extremely attractive woman. She has raven-black hair and bright-black eyes and high cheekbones. She's also the only doctor I've ever consulted who wore fashionable cowboy boots. Black.

Finished, she offered the likely reason for the new pain. As bones wear away, they take note of what's happening and set about to grow themselves back to what they'd been. This seems to me a commendable effort—a spirit of can-do self-reliance about it. But it's also a crude and clueless one, a random calcium misfiring that causes bone spurs to sprout most anywhere, congregating, say, at the back of the knee, just where my throbbing was. So if the pristine knee is a lovely sculptural assemblage, an aging knee trying valiantly, haplessly to repair itself makes an artless mess of things.

Some while ago I read a piece in the *New York Times* that described a hideous example of the effort our bones make on our behalf. They are "ambitiously, tirelessly alive," wrote Natalie Angier. They are in a sense "more animate than the muscles and fat draped over [them] . . . certainly more attuned to [their] surroundings." But in the case of a man named Harry Eastlack, his bones were *unrestrainedly* attuned. As a boy, Harry Eastlack's body worked to repair every one of the childhood "cuts, bruises and trauma" it received. And how did it go about making these repairs? By growing new bone. Before he was ten, bony deposits had appeared on his chest, on his neck, on his back and buttocks. When surgeons removed them, they returned, denser, thicker. Over the next dozen years, his vertebrae fused—the muscles of his back replaced with bone. Ultimately, wildly vigorous new bone attached itself everywhere to his skull, preventing his jaw from opening, and he died of pneumonia at thirty-nine from a congenital disease called fibrodysplasia ossificans progressiva. His skeleton was entombed in the skeleton it had grown.

And yet, couldn't you also say that Harry Eastlack's bones meant well? That they had the purest of intentions as they went about their Good Samaritan and finally lethal work?

In Dr. Matzkin's exam room, she confirmed what I'd already assumed—that there was knee-replacement surgery in my future. Ideally, she said, a decade or so in my future, maybe even longer if I were lucky and continued to exercise, exercise, keeping the muscles surrounding the joint as strong as possible. Then she asked, of my medial-meniscusless knee, "What happened, by the way? How did you first hurt it?"

"Oh," I said, "it's a long story."

ॐ

The long story:

Marvin Winegar was, at seventeen, a tree trunk of a young man, with a big, round face and a crewcut as flat as a just-trimmed hedge. His gait was a rhythmic side-to-side rocking, his legs bowed, his massive chest leading like a prow. He was a brute whose brutishness contained an amiable sweetness, his smile warm and benedictory when he passed you in the hall or walked with you from the locker room to football practice.

When I was Marvin's high school teammate, I didn't see his tick-tock stride as the first sign of what was not quite yet a limp, the result of serial injuries to one of his knees. Instead I saw it as the way you got to walk if your nickname was Hoss, as Marvin's was, a nickname you had earned, as Marvin had, because of the violent joy with which you knocked people down on a football field, as Marvin did. As a boy I was an especially vivid fantasist, and as this story will show I carried the tendency into adolescence, and much beyond. For me, Hoss was mesmerizing evidence that bearing an injury—or even better, playing with it, playing through it—defined a kind of lonely valor, a greater grit, a more textured courage.

An indelible moment on an autumn Friday night: The field lights silvering the frost-crusted grass. Beyond the end zones and the goalposts, harvested cornfields disappearing into the Iowa night. The few sections of bleachers on either side of the field were sparsely filled, since those who really cared—a third, sometimes as much as half the crowd—stood close to the side-lines behind a field-long length of snow fence, and moved back and forth with the action to keep the play in front of them.

I was standing, too, at our bench with the other reserves, when I spotted Hoss hop-skipping off the field and pointing to his fragile knee. Seeing him, our coach ordered a substitute into the game as he hurried to meet Hoss and help him to the bench.

Coach McAllister was a small man, short, very short, but thick-necked and muscular. His first name was Jerry. Behind his back we called him "Jerry Babe," not out of disrespect but with amused affection. To us, he was an exotic figure. We'd somehow come to know that he was an ex-Marine, though it's hard to imagine he met the height requirement, and his coaching voice was a bark that rose to an excited squeak when his team did something very right or very wrong. It was a voice you could easily imagine screaming at the newly enlisted.

The other exotic thing about him was his right index finger, almost all of which was gone. No one would have dared ask him about it. By consensus we attributed it to an act of battlefield heroism in Korea. His trigger finger blown off in the taking of Pork Chop Hill.

All to say that it was extremely cool to have a coach who was a tiny ex-Marine with an ugly stub of an index finger.

Reaching the sidelines, Hoss dropped to the ground and lay on his back while Jerry Babe knelt down and together they hastily unbuckled the elaborate brace Hoss wore. Jerry Babe had a few times blown his whistle to stop practice and tend to Hoss after he'd hit someone and his knee slipped out of joint. But it hadn't happened in a game, under the lights, in front of a crowd, which made those previous occasions dress rehearsals of a kind.

They exchanged "Ready? Ready." nods, then Jerry Babe gave a practiced pull and Hoss's knee clicked back into place.

Whole again, he hurriedly strapped his brace back on, jumped up, and ran out to rejoin the play.

Behind me, a cluster of local men laughed appreciatively.

"You see that? Bastard popped up like a jack in the box."

"His goddamn guts, they had ten more like him . . ."

"Ten? I'd do with two or three."

It says everything about what I wished to be and wasn't that I saw Jerry Babe bending down to tend to Hoss as something deeply fraternal, as the way wounded warriors acknowledged one another, the two of them speaking a private language of fluent nods; a wordless diction of goddamn guts.

I wanted Hoss's knee.

Earlier that season, I'd been tangled up in a pile in a blocking drill when my left knee gave, then snapped back into alignment. What I felt inside an entirely new degree of pain was the quick abrasion of grinding parts. "Get off!" I yelled. "Get off! Get off!"

I got to my feet as Jerry Babe trotted over and asked me if I was all right. The knee had already begun to stiffen.

I said I was.

He nodded and told me to sit out the rest of practice.

I was kept from scrimmages for a few days while the swelling subsided. Then I returned to my role as the slow-footed second-team quarterback. And that was that. Whatever had happened to my knee, it was far from enough to earn the little ex-Marine's fraternal attention.

I twice re-injured it in high school—wrestling in gym class, playing pickup basketball. Both times, as with the first, there was that shock of how much it hurt for just an instant, then as quickly everything popped back into place.

After the episode on the basketball court, my parents drove me into Des Moines to see a specialist. From the distance of more than forty years, I don't remember the doctor's name or what he looked like, but my memory sees him clearly: middle-aged, five feet ten or so, stocky, a slight paunch, and baldish, emphasizing his egg-shaped head. I'll call him Dr. Leonard.

"It's the medial meniscus," Dr. Leonard said, pointing to the X-ray. He told me I was lucky there was no ligament damage. He said the tears should heal as good as new so long as I didn't hurt my knee further.

When my final football season came and I was at last the starting quarterback, I wore a supportive pad around the knee. I call it supportive, and I told myself it was, even as I knew it was only a standard-issue knee pad, a rectangle of foam rubber inside a wide band of red elastic fabric, nothing like the elaborate scaffolding that supported the now-graduated Hoss's knee. In truth I wore the pad not because I believed my knee was more than slightly at risk. Dressing for practices and games, I made sure some of the red elastic showed below the leg of my white football pants because I wanted Jerry Babe to see it and be reminded that I'd hurt my knee and yet continued to play. I wanted those who came to our games and moved up and down the sidelines, watching for a bastard with some goddamn guts, I wanted them to see that band of red elastic and think that I was playing with a chronic injury.

Most of all, I wanted Louise to see it from where she stood near the bleachers with the other cheerleaders in their scarlet and black outfits.

We'd been dating for a year. She was a petite brunette with a wide, unavoidably flirtatious smile. To say that ours was nothing more than the usual adolescent ardor is of course to say that it was something febrile. And yet night after night we managed to stop at the last, and I mean last, moment, panting, sweating, with most of our clothes—and on some ecstatic occasions all of Louise's—scattered on the floor around the couch. Our sense of right and wrong contested agonizingly with our urges, and in its way it was as visceral. It was a moral weather we couldn't escape.

In the last game of that last season I called a play that assigned me, with other blockers, to lead our running back on a sweep around the end. Which I did, hurling myself toward an opponent's chest as bodies converged, and when the tackle had been made and everyone else got up I lay on the ground, turned away from our sidelines, fetally tucked into myself.

The impulse had come to me as I was disappearing among the arms and legs and great rude grunts, and as I lay there I was imagining the crowd's attention, particularly Louise's as she watched intently, her fingertips pressed to her mouth, worry creasing her beautiful high forehead.

The referee stood over me, seeing my hands cupping my crotch. "Get it in the jewels?" he asked.

Through a wince—surely the appropriate affect—I managed, faintly, "Yeah."

Why did my instinct go *there*? And particularly, why not my knee? Did I carry the memory of Hoss hurrying off the field as the example I couldn't tarnish? Did I consider my knee and its history of injury to be honorable and true, however modest? I'd like to think that either might be so. Far more likely in that instant I thought without thinking that my knee swelled and stiffened immediately when I hurt it and how would I explain the fact that it wasn't?

The referee looked to our sidelines and I could not believe how loudly he shouted, "Just his jewels!"

I lay there thinking, *Just?*

"Hop up, son," he said, his voice amused. "We've got a football game to play."

Bastard popped up like a jack in the box.

Having never gotten it in the jewels, I had no idea of the half-life of its pain, how much I should still be feeling. But I couldn't imagine I'd be able to pop up like a jack-in-the-box, so I got slowly to my feet and, turning to greet Jerry Babe arriving to escort me from the field, I saw him standing in front of our bench, from where he clearly hadn't moved, propellering his hand, motioning me to hurry off.

I settled on a kind of sputtering jog/stagger and headed off, glimpsing as I did the cheerleaders clustered closely. I couldn't make out Louise's expression.

"You'll be good in a minute," Jerry Babe said, not unsympathetically, when I reached him. As always, his authority was absolute, suggesting that as a tiny Marine he'd gotten it in the jewels countless times and it was no big deal. I took his cue, waited a short while, then told him I felt fine. He nodded and sent me back in to finish the game, which we lost: 12 to 6 if memory serves.

I was driving Louise home afterward, a distance of six or seven blocks. She sat thrillingly close as she always did in that golden age before bucket seats.

"I'm sorry about the game," she said.

"Thanks," I said, "me too."

Several months later, Louise would travel to Hawaii to spend the summer with her much older brother, who'd moved there years before, after his divorce. And when she returned at summer's end she would explain to me that her time away had shown her paradisiacal evidence that the world was vast and it was waiting and she needed to feel she could find it on her own. Her voice in telling me this would be unassailably calm. And while I could grieve—and I would; I did; I was devastated—the sound of her brand-new worldliness would make it clear that nothing I might say had a chance against the impatient certainty of a very bright young woman from a tiny town in landlocked Iowa who'd just crisscrossed the ocean.

But that heartbreak was months away and on this night, as I said, we were sitting thigh to thigh while I waited for Louise to ask me how I felt. Finally I asked, "So were you worried?"

"Worried?"

"Yeah . . . when I got hurt?"

She would have had to slide toward her door in order to turn and face me directly. So she was looking straight ahead into the empty small-town night when she said, "Oh. Did you get hurt?"

The ballroom was a mass of spastic choreography, and somewhere in the middle of it, drunk and happy, my shirt sodden with sweat, I was a Famous Flame, a Temptation, one of Smokey's Miracles with my double-Dutch footwork and high prance steps. Carol, small and blonde and cherub-cheeked, was dancing alongside me but I was rudely with the music, and when the singer and the horns hit the pulsing refrain—"Devil with the blue dress, blue dress, blue dress / Devil with the blue dress on"—then drums cascading, I gathered myself and jumped into the air.

Drunk as I was, I probably got about six inches off the floor. But in the better truth of memory I am high in the air and helium-light. The instant is silent and I possess, at the age of twenty-one, an overseer's wisdom as, floating, suspended, I survey the crowded Val-Air Ballroom, the same room where my mother and father, elegantly in love, came to dance when they were courting and engaged.

I was in the air and then I was sitting on the hardwood floor with no sense of having landed and my knee buckling, and anes-thetized by booze I was aware of no pain, none.

I sat there, blinking and confused, looking up at a handful of fraternity brothers and their dates gathering around me. Carol was bending down to me, her beautiful long hair falling forward, blondly hooding her face. She asked, concerned, if I were all right. She was smiling. My roommate, Nick, looked down to ask me if I could stand. I nodded and reached my arm toward him, like to a teammate after making a tackle, and let him help me up. By now the circle had become a small crowd and my sheepish grin was obvious and everyone knew that it was fine to laugh in the way we laugh at the banana peel slip, the vaudeville spill.

When I'd hurt the knee before, the pain and the swelling had pretty much disappeared after ten days or so. But not this time. Finally, I went to see Dr. Leonard again, who asked, "How did it happen?"

How did it happen? Well, there was this party before the dance and I drank way too much and I really love Mitch Ryder and the Detroit Wheels . . . Could it have been less valorous? Less heroic? Could my knee have been less Hoss-like?

"I fell," I said.

"Well," he said, "I'm afraid you've really done it."

‿ʒ⁊

I want to freeze that fiction of myself afloat in the ballroom air, and recall some things I didn't know would be coming once I landed.

Still in the air, I hadn't yet lived the early summer night, five months after surgery had removed the cartilage. It was a night too hot for the window fans to help, with the smell of sautéing onions likely coming up from Gladys's, the landlady's, apartment below, because she sautéed onions cooking supper almost every night, and I sat on my living room floor, sweating and grunting, my right leg fully extended, my left bent back under me as far possible, putting all the pressure I could on my recently repaired knee.

The letter ordering me to report at six o'clock the next morning to the Fort Des Moines Army Base for my pre-induction physical exam had come some weeks before. If I passed I'd be drafted and surely sent to Vietnam.

I had not, as had some of my college friends, planned for how to meet the awful dilemma of the war by applying early for admittance into their state's National Guard. I had not decided, as others had, that the life we all were facing would be measurably better as an officer, which meant the hard, considered choice of Officer Candidate School. I had not sat down, nor had anyone I knew, to map my route to Canada.

To the question of what to do about the likelihood of Vietnam, the sum and substance of my plan had been to take a drunken tumble at a fraternity dance six months before graduation, tear a great deal of weakened cartilage in a knee that had been otherwise free of injury for three years, then have the cartilage surgically removed and hope that the knee would disqualify me from the draft.

That night, on my apartment floor, as I lay arranging and rearranging my body, I was not a foolish high school boy publicly pretending I was hurt to win the admiration of the culture and the concern of the girl I loved to distraction. I was a terrified young man truly trying to hurt myself, while wildly imagining the morning to come: me among hundreds in a perversely orchestrated chaos, clustered in the rooms and filing down the hallways of Fort Des Moines, all of us being cursed and ridiculed, ordered here and there by soldiers shouting Jerry Babe screams that rose to squeaks like mad crows', until hours later, clutching papers stamped Approved, I'd be herded onto a bus and driven away to God knows where with the other inductees from the small towns of our sparsely populated county whose draft board was desperate to fill its monthly quotas, and not one of them showing the fear I would be trying and failing to hide, as if the daily goddamn gutsiness of their lives had fully prepared them.

On the floor of my seedy apartment that night I pushed to force my knee to do what it had done four times before: to come loose with that feeling like gristle grinding and the instant of pain ridiculous, except for the last time when I was so drunk I'd felt none. My left leg still bent under me, I leaned back, breathing hard to take me as far as I could get, not from pain I remembered but from the pain I was making, till I lay nearly supine to put still more stress on the knee. But no matter how I lay, I got nothing to tear, nothing to give way. My knee, meaning well, with the purest of intentions, stayed maddeningly secure.

The next morning a requisitely surly Army doctor tugged and pulled at my knee before deciding it was unfortunately too unstable. He would have to let me go free today, ordering me to return in three months.

It failed that second examination as well. And it failed a third, six months after the second. I was as frightened the second morning as I'd been the first and no less so the third. And each time I reported I was handed a fresh stack of forms. Over the course of these three pre-induction physicals I built a file that became, truly, as thick as a major city phone book.

"What the hell is this?" the doctor set to examine me the third time said as I handed over my massive file. I still hear his contempt and still see his snarl, and I fully believe that, as much as the question of my knee's soundness, it was that stack of paperwork he thought he'd have to wade through that moved him, brooding almost audibly, to dismiss me.

I never heard from the Army again.

Still in the air before my oafish dance-floor fall, I didn't know that roughly three years later Carol and I would marry, and that we'd be very happy for a time. Until we moved to Chicago, for each of us our first real city, where we began to recognize that the world was boundless—the very news Louise had brought me from Hawaii—and that we'd seen little of it, and in a mood of fear and sadness and an exhilaration we tried to keep from one another we agreed that we could best begin to see it on our own.

That night, still in the air, I didn't know that in my early thirties I'd begin to run three or four miles a day to get in better shape. I'd lose some weight I did not gain back so that I was no longer the slow-as-a-dray-horse high school athlete. And I divined an equation that has lasted me for decades: my new quickness was proof, despite my knee, of my invulnerable youthfulness. If I couldn't be Hoss-brave, at least I could be fast on the tennis court forever while wearing a now entirely necessary brace, not a red elastic pad. And then one day—and it really did seem that sudden: one day—the joint began to stiffen when it hadn't and hurt where it hadn't, so I went to see Dr. Matzkin, who wondered how I could be walking, and who told me to play until I couldn't and then I'd get a new knee, a gleaming, special-ordered factory part, which, as I write, I haven't needed yet to order.

From where I sit now, from inside my body now, I'm forty years late in accepting the grown-up truth that my injured knee confers no lonely valor, no status as an injury to play through. Age has redefined it simply as creeping decrepitude. If we are lucky, we live some tolerable, slowly incremental version of Harry Eastlack's hideous ill fortune: our bodies release us into active physical life and steadily, gradually close us off from it. If, as I say, we are lucky.

That night, still suspended in the ballroom air, I didn't know that twelve years would pass until the afternoon I answered my telephone to hear Louise say hello and identify herself, which she didn't need to do for her voice in my ear was as if we'd agreed the night before to speak again tomorrow. I didn't know that two months after her call I would come from my home in upstate New York and she from hers in Italy, to meet in Washington, D.C., where she was staying with friends. That for me our meeting was an escape from a fast-failing relationship and for her part of a trip to the States for other, necessary reasons, not an escape from her marriage, which wasn't failing.

That night we would at last make love, our bodies both seeking and noting, knowing and new, wanting to complete all the times we'd stopped, wanting to include all the time since then. Afterwards she would tell me she'd often been tempted to find me. When I'd say I was surprised, given how we ended, she'd say she understood, but ask me to consider that she had just turned seventeen.

I'd remind her, not angrily, that I was seventeen too, which meant that during that summer she was gone, everything I thought and felt was one thing: she was gone. And then she came back and I found out she still was.

Dawn would bring near-light through the bedroom curtains, letting us again begin to see, as well as touch and talk to, one another, and at some point she would absently trace the scar on my knee, a plump-worm-looking line suggesting slapdash violence, and today, its pinkness faded, camouflaged among the dimples of my aging flesh, all but invisible.

"Is this how you got out of Vietnam?" she'd ask. "Your knee?"

Her husband had gone to Officer Candidate School. And after Vietnam, having chosen the Army as his career, they were living in Rome with their two children, where Louise, speaking fluent Italian, was supervising a domestic and social staff, which came with his assignment as a high-ranking military attaché.

Only a moment would pass before I answered her question. But a moment is more than time enough for two histories to step forward and present themselves like soldiers for inspection.

"Yes," I'd say. "My knee."

WHAT WE HUNGER FOR

ᘓ

IN THE SPRING OF 1971, I WAS WORKING AS A LOWLY EDITOR at *Playboy* when the executive editor called me into his office. Sitting behind his desk, a thin, perennially agitated man wreathed as always in cigarette smoke, he excitedly announced that M.F. K. Fisher was going to write a piece for the magazine on New Orleans food and restaurants. He saved me from saying, "M.F. K. Fisher? Who's he?" by relaying her one demand. She'd told him she would need a cohort for her time in New Orleans. If she were to visit any restaurant unaccompanied and anonymous she'd instantly be steered to the room's Siberia, the dark corner by the kitchen, behind the aspidistra.

I understand, the editor had told her. And I know just who to send to accompany you. A very bright young woman, the new star of our staff.

No, no, she'd said. Two women would suffer an identical fate. The dark corner. The aspidistra. The crashing cymbal-sounds of pots and pans every time the kitchen door swung open. Her companion must be male.

The executive editor added, laughing, "She told me, 'I don't care what sex he is, as long as he wears pants.'"

I did, still do, wear pants, and fairly expertly if I do say so. But this was the extent of my qualifications. I was almost twenty-six years old, had recently moved to Chicago from Des Moines, and I would bring to the task of M.F.K. Fisher's dining partner exactly no sophistication regarding food (or anything else). My idea of an accompanying sauce was ketchup.

"I am, as often, tempted to start a personal book," Mary Frances Kennedy Fisher wrote in her journal, on the fourth of March, 1937, "mais a quoi bon? I think my present life is a strange, complicated, interesting one. But my deep distrust—or is it timidity, cowardice even?—of such self-revelations will, perhaps, always prevent me from thus relieving myself."

She'd left California the previous fall with her husband, Al Fisher, to share a house in a vineyard above the Swiss village of Vevey, with its owner, their friend, the painter Dillwyn Parrish, whom everyone called by his nickname, Timmy. And by the following early spring, when she made this journal entry, her marriage was ending, Al was returning to the States to teach at Smith, and Mary Frances was about to return as well, but only briefly, to tell her parents she was divorcing Al Fisher and marrying Timmy Parrish and that the two of them would continue on together in Vevey. A strange, complicated, interesting life indeed.

She was twenty-eight years old in 1937, just two years older than I was the day I learned in my ignorance that we were about to meet. It was also the year she published her first book, *Serve It Forth*. Like the majority of her writing—more than twenty books, most of them, to borrow one of her titles, devoted to "the art of eating"—it speaks in anecdotal glimpses of cooking and dining and living with her senses as her guide.

In Vevey, she and Timmy Parrish had nearly a year of idyllic life. He painted. She wrote. They ambitiously gardened. They entertained their rustic neighbors and loved doing so. And then Parrish got sick with what proved to be Buerger's disease, a rare illness of the veins and arteries in the arms and legs. He was in great pain and a first operation made it greater and a second, to amputate his left leg, left him suffering even more.

The following year they moved back to California, to a crumbling house in the Mojave Desert. They called it Bareacres. In her journal she speaks of the barren beauty of the landscape and of plans for expanding the house. But more and more their life became his illness and their efforts to solve it. Of clinics visited, of medicines tried.

Until this journal entry, on September 3, 1941: "I drink a too-hot, too-strong toddy in bed, and if my luck holds I get to sleep after some dutiful trash reading. . . . [A]bout one morning out of three or four, I sleep heavily until 8:00 or so without hearing the shot. I try to live (even asleep?) with what dignity I can muster, but I wonder if there is much in this abject procedure."

Four weeks earlier, Parrish had at last found a way to solve his pain, going from life into death in the time it took the bullet.

Her youngest sister, Norah, wrote of her, "Mary Frances, of course, had to live on, day by day, after the loss of her love . . . and she was very much a person who continued to love and be loved during her long productive life."

She certainly did live on, eventually marrying again and subsequently divorcing, raising two daughters, and writing prolifically about it all, with food as the axis around which matters of deeper life revolve. And a hallmark of that work is the way she shared her life with such artful obliqueness, her depictions of the people and places in it glancingly referred to, beguilingly allusive.

In a piece she wrote for *Holiday* in 1956: "On that night I watched him sitting at a wobbly card table in my new apartment amidst a mess caused by the arrival of most everything I own from Aix-en-Provence, where I had stayed a year." Why Aix? Why a year? Returning to where? Who's "him"?

This just might be the prototypical Fisher sentence, with its picture of her living modestly, making do with no apology, serving her guest at a wobbly card table; but also living an enviable, international, and—to her readers, particularly women, in the 1940s, '50s, '60s, even into the '70s—a fantastical life. *I'd just returned from a year in Aix-en-Provence.*

Coming down the stairs from her room to meet me in the hotel lobby, she extended her hand and offered me a warm smile and spoke in her surprisingly small, melodiously high voice, of the great adventure we were about to embark on. She was a tall woman, and in her early sixties somewhat stout and quite beautiful, as she had been and would be all her life. Photos of her through the decades record an early ingenuous film-star glamour, truly, and a late wise, delicate loveliness.

Which is to say, among other things, that she brought with her to New Orleans more than enough sophisticated knowledge of food and of the world for both of us. But she wore her sophistication lightly, offered it easily. I felt that lightness and ease right away and with them the invitation to be myself.

We quickly devised an excellent strategy, one we held to through the week. Wherever we dined, Mary Frances would scan the menu and decide what dishes we should order and what wine we should drink and when the waiter came I would tell him what she'd just told me. Hence, we fell naturally into the roles for which we were suited. And whether lunch or dinner, whether fancy or plain, each time I'd finished ordering I looked around, not an aspidistra in sight, and knew I wasn't in Des Moines any more.

For a week, our days followed this sublime routine. After mornings on our own, we met in the lobby and headed out to lunch. Then we separated again, reconvened each night at the hotel bar, and before venturing to dinner, drank a Ramos gin fizz. It was a drink, I needn't tell you, I was unfamiliar with. I think I recall us watching the hotel bartender deftly mixing one and, what with an egg white and cream among its ingredients, maybe we decided it was close enough to food. We'd be shirking our assignment not to taste one. In any case, we decided, a kind of gustatory side bet, that part of our New Orleans exploration would be to find the city's best Ramos gin fizz.

With every dish of every meal, Mary Frances looked across the table and, her mood entirely professional, asked me, "What do you think?" And, "Tell me how it tastes." What an enormous act of charity this was, inspiring me to concentrate on what I was eating as I never had. I chewed with the thoroughness of a Fletcherite, trying to identify flavors as she furtively slipped her notebook out of her purse to jot things down.

I think the vast chasm of knowledge and life experience and the forty years of age that separated us was so comfortably bridged because, at the *heart* of who we were, we shared a Midwest temperament. Mary Frances was born in a small town in Michigan. Her beloved father, Rex, was, like me, raised in Iowa. Yes, we understood we'd be in one another's company for a week no matter what, but something more than self-preservation was at work. For me, I felt as the week progressed her awarding me what I can only call her validation. It's a generosity I still find remarkable. For again and again in our conversations, I heard her genuine curiosity in asking, *What do you think?* Heard her interest in wondering what I thought, not just about food, but about life. And then, about my own, *How does it taste?* So prompted, I spoke at least as often about my pitifully few and untraveled years as she did about her incredibly eventful ones.

We talked a lot about what was for both of us a time of moving into new lives. Mine in Chicago. Hers in her new house—a white stone cottage tucked in hillocky Sonoma valley pastureland—which she called with characteristically provocative candor, Last House.

As her life played out, it was in fact in her bedroom in that house where she died twenty years later. But she christened it Last House as it was being built not primarily with the thought that it was where she wished to end her days, but where she could most richly *live* them. And indeed they were twenty vibrant, populated, incredibly productive years.

After my father died, with the farmhouse he and my mother had lived in for nearly sixty years sold, she moved to a small apartment in the nearby town of Newton. She'd hoped to find a place to rent in Prairie City, her home village, but there was nothing available. Then, six months later, she got word that something was and she moved again, to a one-bedroom apartment in a brick single-story duplex at the extreme northeast corner of the town where a short street of houses meets the fields. Pleased as she was to be back among her intimate friends—few as there were still living—and the merchants she knew, and the Methodist church that was now twelve small-town blocks, not twelve miles, away, she worried at first that she'd made a great mistake.

The long shotgun apartment she'd rented shared a common wall with its twin and she was concerned that the noises she would hear and be conscious of making might compromise her privacy. More than that, she was dismayed by the sense of grime and gloom the place gave off, and here my brother, who'd driven up from St. Louis to take a look, assured her that freshly painted white walls would change the feel completely. The following weekend, with his wife and their three sons, they set about to do precisely that. Two days later, the apartment was transformed.

Leaving the huge country house, she'd pared her possessions dramatically, but with the furniture she'd kept the place felt neither too crowded nor too spare. I got the sense when I spent time there, recognizing the couch, the easy chairs, the dining room hutch, the bedroom chest of drawers, that I was visiting a miniature replica of the farmhouse rooms.

I felt this especially in her kitchen, perhaps a third as large as the one on the farm where, for better and worse, she'd mostly lived for more than fifty years. I recognized the darkly stained colonial table and chairs, the narrow metal cabinet where she kept all her pantry goods, the plates and cups and tableware, the large stoneware jar she filled with her addictive oatmeal cookies when her grandsons were coming to visit the farm—the jar, she complained, they emptied like heathens much too quickly, requiring her to bake another batch and then another. I saw the electric frying pan she'd used for decades, in which, after slicing a tomato, she would be frying bacon for a supper sandwich on a hot August night in 2008 and would turn and lose her balance and fall, breaking her left hip, then begin a painful twelve-hour crawl to reach her telephone.

The one addition to this kitchen was a long wooden cabinet with a Formica top and several drawers. It was built for her by a nephew-in-law who noticed, when visiting, that the kitchen lacked counter and storage space. She'd asked him to paint it a brilliant blue, a bold departure from her usual beige and brown muted tones. She seemed inordinately pleased with the color, pointing it out right away and asking people their opinion, as if it were proof that she wasn't so predictable at this stage of her life as folks might assume.

Otherwise, everything in the new kitchen was the farm's. Even the window above the sink looked east, as the farm's had, and also gave onto a quietly gradient field, the lay of land she most admired, that ran for several acres, alternating corn and soybeans year to year.

The view to the north from her living room picture window was another matter. Directly across the street stood a large blond-brick one-story structure that had been built, and served for many years, as the town's nursing home. It had been recently reopened as a residence for women who were about to become, and in some cases were, single mothers with very meager means of support.

But in my mind, and my mother's, it was the nursing home. Several of her friends died there. Her mother-in-law died there. It was for years where the majority of Prairie City went to die. Now it was her picture window view, directly across the street.

And something more. Though she couldn't see it from her window, just two short blocks farther north lay the local cemetery and the gravestone that was now my father's and would also be hers.

More than thirty years ago, when I returned to the town to live for a time and write a book about it, I observed that people who live their whole lives in such small places must deal with a terribly intimate topography. Memory and moment and future, all of them are embedded and overlapping. Obviously, the passing of years separates the beginnings of lives from their present ones and their present from what's to come. But the place, the physical place, is at every stage the same. It seemed to me then, and does still, that a certain frame of mind—a particular courage—is required to live comfortably enough in a single landscape that holds your past, your present, your future. The more local your life, the more you look at the details of your ending.

She was a churchgoer all her life. She taught Sunday School now and then through the years and sang in the choir, and, particularly after she was widowed, the church's activities were her axis. She was one of a group of women who worked in the church kitchen, most of them only slightly younger than she and, like her, showing their histories in their faces, their lines of age like webbings of soft scars. They served the luncheons routinely eaten after funerals in the big open room the church called Fellowship Hall. They served ham sandwiches on soft hamburger buns stacked on platters in high pyramids; gelatin salads in every shade of orange and red and green; cake cut into rectangles as big as bricks; weak coffee you could almost see through to the bottom of your cup. Surely my mother, helping so often over so many years, looked out from behind the serving counter into that big open room, her cordial sadness no less genuine for being regularly called upon, and pictured the day it would be filled with *her* family and friends, as indeed it was the day of her service, all of us eating the sandwiches and gelatin and cake she might have served us.

When she moved to her apartment, she made it clear that it was the last place she would live unaided. During those nearly seven years she was seriously ill more than once—a heart attack, pneumonia, assorted maladies—and each time she returned home from the hospital there came the conversation about the ease and wisdom of her moving to a place where she'd have, in the hideous euphemism, continuing care. More than once, I strongly urged her, and more than once she seemed ready. But each time, she balked and decided she would stay until it was obvious she couldn't. She pledged she wouldn't be a burden, but said what she hoped was that she would simply and suddenly drop dead in the apartment.

She nearly got what she hoped for. Except for those handful of hospital stays, she lived there until ten days before she died, looking east to the fields and north to the nursing home and, in her mind, two blocks farther to the final earth she'd own. And I wonder if her picture window view helped to strengthen her resolve that she'd come to her last apartment not to die but to live as well as she could. To remind her when she looked across the street of the kind of place she didn't want to be her last.

In New Orleans, did I come to view Mary Frances as in some way maternal, a surrogate of sorts? I'm sure I did, maybe inevitably. But if so, it was not a notion I was conscious of. Instead, I saw her as someone whose example made it clear that we can fully celebrate our appetites—for food, yes, but for love, for festivity, for smaller daily pleasures—once we know that life approves of our having them. This was not a message I recognized as remotely maternal.

Over the years, as a convenient symbol of their differences, I invoked the landscapes of Iowa and wine-valley California, grain fields and vineyards, which have so much in common and, in their purpose, so much that contrasts them. I thought, as I often do, of my mother's admiration for a field that was clean, neat, her aesthetic one of an abstinent order. I compared that with what I assumed Mary Frances saw in a vineyard—order, yes, the hand-pruned rows, the lovely lines in the land; but finally the grapes and the pleasure they appeal to. I thought of the words *restraint* and *allowance*; the fear of indulgence and the alertness of the senses.

As for Mary Frances, in her first correspondence after New Orleans, she began, "Dear Favorite Iowa Farm Boy." Her letters over the years would always, somewhere in them, jokingly insist that that is what I was, her favorite Iowa farm boy and, yes, there's something undeniably maternal in that.

I said she included the phrase as a fond joke, and it was. But I also came to read it as her way of reminding me that I would continue to move further and further away from what I'd been. But, now and always, where I began was who I was and what a foolish waste of energies if I tried not to be.

Wherever we walked that week, whether to Preservation Hall to hear the geriatric jazz band or to the Café Du Monde to eat its famous beignets, I got used to her coming to an abrupt stop when something caught her attention. She said she'd always been an unapologetic gawker and she often stood for quite a long time, not ready to move on until she'd taken in completely what it was she was looking at.

One night on Bourbon Street she came to such a stop at the sight of a woman's legs suddenly swinging out into the night, then back through a high open window of a strip club. Mary Frances watched the stripper on her swing appear and disappear and appear again for several seconds before saying, "How beauti-ful." Her tone was purely appreciative of those lovely white legs tracing their pendular arc in the night-lit sky.

All week long, she took in everything that way, ready simply to *receive* the sense of the experience, and I saw that the way to be curious about the life of a place was to wander and watch and to look with no apology for as long as it takes to understand what you're seeing.

Before my mother's funeral there was a family graveside service. At its end the pastor, Reverend Riggle, asked us to join him in prayer. In it, he described the moment of God receiving her and taking her into His welcoming hands. Standing in an outlandish January cold with my partner, Sue, and my brother and his family, I imagined knowledgeable guides meeting a traveler. I pictured my mother being handed off from some mortal agent—Reverend Riggle? Why not?—to a Heavenly deputy come down to escort her the rest of the way.

I envisioned this transfer taking place on a New York subway platform, of her being guided from the local to the express side at 42nd Street. It was a place on the planet where, in fact, she had once stood, on a stifling, steaming summer day in 1982, weather as opposite from the morning of her funeral as it is possible for weather to be, the subway tunnel foul with fumes and hot as a Bessemer.

I was acting as the tour guide for her and my father, showing them around Manhattan on their first and only visit to New York. And hot as it was, they were eager, avid tourists. They showed no serious signs of flagging through the day, and we saw a *lot* of the island over the course of several hours, from Central Park to the Upper East Side, then back to Midtown and west to 10th Avenue to a favorite casual restaurant of mine I thought they would enjoy because it had been thoroughly restored to its turn-of-the-century splendor. To get there we walked several blocks past buildings that were, in 1982, badly derelict, along sidewalks considerably littered with trash and drunks. For years afterward, my father spoke of that walk, recalling the startling urban dystopia. He spoke as well, even more keenly, of our reaching the restaurant and, sweating strongly from the heat, ordering three Heinekens at the U-shaped wooden bar. "Best beer I ever drank in my life," he always said, smiling at the recollected pleasure of his first sip.

We ended the day on a restaurant patio in Greenwich Village.

My mother looked around, enchanted by the strings of tiny white lights that lit the finally cooling night, and said, "I can't believe I'm sitting here having dinner in Greenwich Village!"

She once told me that, as a young girl growing up in Colfax, Iowa, she'd believed that the streets of New York were literally paved with gold. Half a century later, finally seeing a place she'd held mythically in her mind for so long must have been something like touring a secular Heaven.

What I remember most from that day was our walk through Central Park. We paused frequently as we strolled, lingering in the welcome shade when we found it. And then at one point as we were walking my mother stopped abruptly in the high hot sun. An incredibly tall, glamorously dressed transvestite was approaching, hurrying toward us with unchecked galumphing strides, like Paul Bunyan in a glittering evening dress late for an appointment. I was aware of my mother staring, yes, *gawking*, in the way a child stares openly while her parent chastises her and futilely explains the rules of social etiquette.

After the transvestite had hurried past, my father said, "Well, you don't see that every day."

And my mother said, "What's so wonderful about New York is, you can be anything you want and nobody's bothered."

When I was clearing her apartment after she died, I found an odd assortment of coins she'd accumulated and kept in a ziplock plastic bag—some shiny Kennedy silver dollars, a couple of pewter-patinated fifty-cent pieces. Included among them was a subway token from that trip—a chip of gold from the streets of New York.

The day Mary Frances and I were leaving New Orleans, we walked late in the morning through the waking Quarter to Felix's and the Acme, the city's celebrated oyster bars. We hadn't visited either one and she felt for the sake of her piece we should. When I told her I'd never eaten raw oysters she declared, "Then we *must*."

We stood at the counter of—I don't remember which place we tried first—and she explained how to let the oyster slide down my gullet so that I would taste the sea. I did as instructed, savoring the briny freshness of flesh too ethereal to be called flesh. After a dozen at each place, turning to leave, we noticed the restaurant directly across the street, a place called Moran's, was opening its doors. Whichever of us suggested it, the other quickly agreed that we should have a last Ramos gin fizz, the drink she'd introduced me to at our hotel bar.

Our search for the perfect one had been in vain. Sometimes the citrus taste was too strong. Sometimes the concoction was shaken too vigorously for too long, so that a sweetish froth of cream and egg white and powdered sugar hid the gin.

Now we entered the restaurant, ordered, watched the bartender's technique, sipped, and wordlessly assessed. Need I say we decided we'd found perfection at Moran's, the ingredients working in balanced harmony, the juniper of the gin like a breeze on the tongue. And part of me knew even then that their excellence had to do with the timing of our drinking them—just as we were about to leave town. Gin fizz perfection at the last second.

When we'd finished, we walked, triumphant, back out into a wet May heat. I waved down a cab and as we strongly hugged I remarked on our morning. A last slow stroll through the Quarter; my first raw oysters; the perfect Ramos gin fizz; and all before noon. It deserved a term of commemoration. What should we call it?

She smiled—in my mind's eye I see both affection and mischief in her expression—and said, "Breakfast, dear Doug. You should call it breakfast."

Of her gifts to me that week, this most explicit suggestion of permission—that life, if we let it, allows us to discover what we're hungry for and when we're hungry for it—is the one that stays most vivid.

We kept in frequent touch for some months after New Orleans, and after that continued to write back and forth less frequently, exchanging notes and letters for a year, two years, then long lapses, then we'd resume. "Now and then," she wrote to me in April 1972, "one meets a person who can last for two months or twenty years and suddenly be there and Time has done more good than harm. I think we are like that. I have a few friends like that in my life."

I remember once rekindling our correspondence after quite a long time with a letter from a hotel in Arles where Sue and I were staying. Mary Frances knew the town and the region intimately and I wrote to tell her I was feeling her presence there. I described the hotel, and the square, and the shaded boulevards. I mentioned our visit to nearby Aix-en-Provence to Cezanne's studio overlooking the town, where, because the space looked working-canvas cluttered, I'd felt *his* presence, too. Shortly after I got home her letter came, saying she had stayed in that hotel forty years before and, as I'd described its view onto the streets, almost certainly the same room. It was the kind of romantic and dubious coincidence she often insisted on, making life's disorderly narrative more artful, more shaped.

Starting in the late '80s, and for several years after, Sue and I happily cheated the end of New England winter, annually renting places for a month or two in Northern California, and on a handful of occasions I got to be in Mary Frances's life again.

I sat one day at her large, round dining table, with six or seven others, members of a television crew who'd come up from San Francisco to interview and film her for a documentary. Though she'd long been admired by an audience of readers, she became in her last years a kind of cult figure, both in the world of food and among a generation of women who saw her life as a model of courageous independence.

We'd talked that morning on the phone and she'd invited me to lunch ("Don't bring any wine. I've got buckets of it") and now I sat in her huge sun-filled room with the television crew, sipping wine and joining the chatter.

Mary Frances was by then very thin and very small, badly crippled by arthritis and Parkinson's disease. She was mostly confined to a wheelchair, able to stand and walk a short distance if she had someone to hold on to. She slipped her arm through yours and gripped it with all her strength. Then she rose up strangely on her toes in her bright pink slippers like a child pretending to dance on point, her heels as high off the ground as she could get them, and, weighing next to nothing, let you drag her forward.

At lunch that day, I watched her presiding at the table. I noticed the penciled-in eyebrows she drew with her unsteady hand rising like profit lines on a corporate chart almost to her temples. She was assembling a large tray of cold cuts, laboriously rolling the ham and salami into tubes and fanning out slices of cheese onto the platter. She'd been talking a lot for the interview and she needed to save what voice she had left. Her Parkinson's greatly weakened it and she often couldn't speak at all after early afternoon. But she was obviously monitoring the conversation closely, smiling at a private thought sparked by something she overheard.

And then she slightly raised her index finger, as though signaling subtly for a waiter's attention, and everyone paused for what she was going to say.

"I want," she whispered hoarsely, "to talk about addictions." Who knew why, perhaps something one of us had said, though the subject seemed to me to have come purely from within her, whatever she'd been thinking, or remembering, or yearning for, and not from anything in the air. "Let's go around the table," she said, "and say what we're addicted to."

The mood among us had been gabby and relaxed and whatever addictions were confessed to came from that same easy attitude.

I was sitting directly across from her and when it was my turn, I admitted that I couldn't claim to have any interesting addictions.

Mary Frances smiled and nodded. "I think that's right. I don't think you do."

"Routine, I guess," I said lamely. "I'm addicted to routine."

She smiled at that, too, and gave the slightest nod, and then the woman whose turn it was also confessed to something safe—M&M's or junk TV—and, after her, someone else did too.

Until it came back around to Mary Frances. She waited a moment, an exactly effective beat, her raconteur's timing as perfect as ever, and whispered, "I used to be addicted to sex." Another perfectly long beat. "Now," she added, "I'm addicted to breathing."

As this luncheon gathering showed, hers was still a life of looking and listening and tasting and describing how she fed herself and others. If age and illness now kept her from venturing out into the world, certainly the world was eager to find its way to her. More than once, I sat with her in her bedroom-office while she answered the constantly ringing phone and listened to someone asking permission to make a pilgrimage—to interview her, to photograph her, to talk with her about her work or about the pilgrim's own.

Yes, come any time, dear, she said. You have priority.

Until the next person called. Yes, of course dear. You have priority.

Her iconic status was one she was happy, I would even say had been impatient, to accept. So, vanity? Yes, of course. But also her undiminished curiosity, its own addiction—her need to learn about the world in ways as small as local gossip, as sweeping as events that had a chance at history. She was as curious about all who came to meet her as she'd been about me, the polite young rube come to New Orleans to be her escort; she wanted to know about their lives; she wanted to know how those lives tasted.

There came a point when my mother no longer felt comfortable driving into Des Moines, twenty miles away, and having to deal with the city traffic. She still drove the Jasper county highways in her big Buick, to Newton and her doctor, to Colfax and her bank. But more and more, she confined her daily errands to the wide, empty village streets, four blocks to the grocery, the post office, to a friend's house, maybe twelve to the church in the opposite corner of the village, as far as one place can be from another in Prairie City and both of them still *be* in Prairie City.

When I've thought about those tiny trips that increasingly met her need, I start with the fact that even at her most energetic, when I was a boy, the farthest she was likely to go, alone or with my father or as a family, was to Des Moines, where there were shops and stores, and where her lively and sarcastically funny older sister, Mable, lived. Her wish to travel even then was satisfied by distances that measure millimeters on a map. I suppose it argues that she was temperamentally suited for a life of nearly instant destinations.

To reach the square, she had to cross a county blacktop that bisected the village north to south. By the standards of a highway its traffic was well-mannered, but it could be loud and formidable—semis bound for the interstate six miles north, tractors high as a house pulling wagons of grain. Also, cars coming into town from the north, slowing a bit but still hurrying through. One day she came to a stop at the blacktop, looked left and right, and pulled out in front of a car that, stating the obvious, she didn't see. Whether the other driver was speeding or not, her car struck my mother's just behind the passenger rear door and sent it into a carnival-ride spin. She emerged unhurt and naturally shaken; the car, the one she owned before the Buick, was irreparably damaged.

She'd driven a car, and excellently, since she bought her beloved Model A at the age of nineteen. In Prairie City, at least when I was growing up there, she had a reputation for the high speeds at which she drove and it was one she enjoyed thoroughly.

Describing her frightening highway accident to me, she was more than a little indignant that the state patrolman called to the scene suggested she might have been at fault in some way.

I can't know about those who grow up in teeming city neighborhoods and stay in them all their lives. But for those of us who *return* to the places of our childhood, we're certain to be struck by their miniature scale. How squat the buildings, how small the spaces, compared to our memories of them. When I was in grade school, the one-block walk from the schoolyard to the square represented a virtual expedition and I remember it taking a *while*—though it patently could not have. There are countless such Prairie City dimensions and distances for me. And once I've left town, they regain their vastness and immensity in my mind until I visit them again.

But the sizes and distances of my mother's local life changed in the opposite way. She drove place to place in a miniscule village that grew larger and more formidable the older she got— four blocks become a continent. Her world was large, not in her memory of living in it as a child but in the moment, larger and larger, due to the mounting challenges of navigating it.

If her universe, seeming vast, in fact got ever smaller, her curiosity in her last years shrank as well. Not much of the world beyond the village came to visit her, and those worlds that might have in books and magazines gave way increasingly to network television and the nightly news from Des Moines of fires and robberies and murders.

She'd always held a deep and knowledgeable interest in politics. She was a liberal Democrat like all her siblings, the children of a coal miner who worshipped John L. Lewis. One of her close friends was a Democrat as well. The *other* one, she liked to say, in her deeply conservative little town. Delighted as she always was in being known as a contrarian, two was just the right number. She had someone with whom to trade sympathetic views.

She loved the rising prominence of the Iowa caucuses. She'd campaigned for Clinton in 1992. She'd caucused for John Edwards in 2004, she liked the handsome ones, and in 2008 she was hoping for Edwards again, though she said she didn't think he had much of a chance.

"But what about Obama?" I asked her. I'd recently sent her a mostly flattering *New Yorker* profile of him. "Did you read the article?"

She shook her head. "No, I can't hack him."

"Really? Why not?"

She said, rendering me wordless, "I think he's a Muslim."

Her arthritic and tremulous hands forced Mary Frances to dictate her thoughts and she seemed to want more than ever to speak to readers. She spent hours sorting through letters and notes, through bulging files and unpublished manuscripts. And also rereading, or having someone read to her, the journals she'd kept over the years, including the one I've quoted here, which became the book *Stay Me, Oh Comfort Me*, published a year after her death. Finally, the world had that personal book she'd thought she should write, and it was the very book in whose pages she'd once written that she was too timid or too cowardly ever to write it. But she was twenty-eight when she wrote those words describing her hesitation, and though—as the beauty of the language in what was then a journal shows—she already possessed the verbal wisdom to convey the hardest matters with a clean brave grace, she was many years away from outliving her timidity or cowardice or whatever else fed her reticence to write fully for readers other than herself.

These entries identify and, in the best sense, exploit her truest subject, which is another kind of hunger than that which she's best known for. It's the hunger to make meaning of one's days when age and illness loom and then descend. This is the hunger that moved her language to a deep, delving, unfussy sensuousness.

In *Stay Me, Oh Comfort Me*, and in *Last House*, another posthumous volume of equally candid considerations, the motive of her prose is not to refer intriguingly to some social episode, but to make transparent sense of much harder stuff.

In a letter to an also aging friend that's included in *Last House*, she says, "Admitting that you are human makes it inevitable that you must admit to growing older, if indeed you are fortunate enough to grow old, and even to deteriorate, disintegrate, fall apart, and finally die. I am very fussy about words, as you know, and here I used the word *fortunate* with great care. I honestly do feel that anyone who can live decently, or even with some difficulty into and past middle age, and then attain old age is lucky."

When my mother died, my brother, who was with her, saw to all the arrangements of her burial. In talking with the funeral director, a kind of checklist in his mind, there was one hard item on it he learned he needn't worry about.

She had written her own obituary, the full and uninflected accounting, as the culture insists (if you can't speak expansively about yourself in life, you certainly can't in death), of names and dates and places, of organizational memberships, and including an abbreviated genealogy.

If you think of the obituary as a genre, it's a kind of imminent press release. *The daughter of John E. and Mary Jane Evans, she was born . . .* Perhaps it's also a wholly personal narrative, a memoirist's in theory, but one rigorously absent all autobiographical embroidery, removing any chance of its having a voice.

Or you could see it as clerical work, a scrivener's task. *She graduated from high school in Colfax . . .* Or, if you write your own obituary, as being the ghostwriter of your own last paper work.

From the first considered phrase to the last punctuation, it is the act of composing life's most intimate essay, composed in a lexicon as dry of intimacy as it's possible for language to be.

It speaks purely to the public, one that, in her case, she knew and could envision many of the faces of. It is, in other words, exactly *not* a journal.

She was preceded in death by her husband, Kenneth . . . To adhere in her prose to that disinterested *she* when, for all the cultural insistence on unadorned facts, the most central of them—the date of her death—was the one she couldn't include. There can be no stronger example of knowing what it is you don't know. How must it have felt while drafting it to confront that place on the page where it would appear in the published version? An obituary must include it, and as its writer she didn't know it, and as the journalist she wasn't, I'm sure she didn't write "[TK]." It seems an act of confirming to yourself, not just that you will die but will die on *a* day among the infinity of days as the indifferent world revolves. But *which* day?

I see her sitting down at her kitchen table, holding a Compliments of the First State Bank of Colfax pen, turning to a fresh page of her spiral notebook, and beginning, her wobbly penmanship betraying her unsteady hand. I work to imagine the emotions of her heart, the focus of her thoughts. I wonder, how easily the writing came.

As she saw it, there was also a practical reality at work. She was faced with an assignment and there was no one else to do it. Her parents and her husband and her siblings were dead, and it's nothing you would dream of asking one of your children to do. The core of her courage was her practicality. Not the courage of a traveler, which would have required a lighter heart, a freer spirit than were hers. But the courage to face some hard domestic duty.

I saw Mary Frances for the last time in the spring of 1992, two months before she died. Sue and I were readying to leave, our month in the wine valleys about to end, and I understood that I would surely not visit Mary Frances again.

She was lying in her bedroom in the hospital bed that had been brought in for her. The work of living had made her even tinier. What I remember noticing, as I sat down beside her, was her long lovely nose in profile, still strong and now disproportionate on her child-sized withered face. That and her eyes, milky and searching, and seeming to be trying, as in New Orleans, to see and understand and hold in her memory whatever she was looking at.

She had only the faint breath of a voice left. I took her hand and told her not to try to talk, an instruction she didn't need or want and weakly waved away. I remembered with her our last New Orleans breakfast. I suppose it's what one does, a sentimental instinct, summon the most memorable occasion. If so, she seemed happy to have it and to lie with it a while. I watched her reach for a plastic glass, a kind of sippy cup, of pineapple juice and labor mightily to get some through a bent plastic straw. A perverse irony of her final days: she, whose finest charm was conversation, whose livelihood was made by tasting food, lost not just her voice but, very near the end, her ability to swallow.

Then she said, a slight exhale of infant sound, "We ate many oysters, didn't we."

A short while later I could see that she was fighting sleep, and I got up and bent down to kiss her forehead.

At the door I stopped and looked back and I saw her hungrily, ravenously, breathing. In my mind's eye, there was something combative, carnal, something lustful, in her effort.

My brother was at our mother's bedside when she died. Later, when I asked him to tell me what he could, his generous letter described entering her room, the nurse stepping forward, telling him she was very close. He described being left alone with her, looking around, trying to imagine the decorum. He described her lunging forward for air, her toothless mouth a baby bird's for food, as the image in its awful beauty came to him.

Mary Frances and my mother. The two of them in desperate unison, become the same as they fought for life as life was leaving them; their gasping lungs; their frantic hearts; fortunate to grow old, disintegrate, and finally die.

IT'S TIME

ↄ

I SAT WITH TWO OTHER PATIENTS IN THE SAME TALL-windowed room where I'd been prepped for my first cataract surgery exactly two weeks before. Across from me, a woman soon to be wheeled away to the operating room was waiting for the intravenous sedatives to take her dreamily. She had a long, bony face and prominent teeth, which sat in her mouth like a double row of tiny backsplash tiles. Separated from her by a curtain sat a man still a bit postsurgically stupid. He was robotically drinking orange juice and eating a blueberry muffin. His head of white hair was mussed as a nest. Tape held a protective patch over his eye, as it had held one over mine two weeks before and very shortly would again.

I recognized the muffin-eating man's state of still-returning consciousness, that stage of recovery when you have the sense that you're observing yourself from some place outside yourself. And watching the woman, her mouth going slack, I recalled the moment of departure as the anesthetics had led me, just as they were leading her, to a luxurious realm of suspended time. So, in looking at these two, I was looking simultaneously at my past and my future and feeling a high-five simpatico, a silly sense of bonhomie. I imagined calling to the man, welcoming him back. I imagined assuring the woman all was going to be fine.

In the weeks before my first surgery, I'd watched website videos of cataracts being removed. I found it pretty absorbing cinema once I got used to seeing micro-sharp needles and blades and beveled tips poking around in someone's eye to a soundtrack of cheesy triumphal music. I'd viewed an ultrasonic stream pulsing through an extremely miniature surgical instrument, a kind of pneumatic drill and vacuum cleaner in combination, which first broke up the lens—the image in the video looked like a thin sheet of ice cracking and fissuring—and then sucked up the fragments.

From some instructional literature I'd learned that there are many subtle variations of this two-step procedure, one that the world of ophthalmic surgery refers to in terms that are unsettlingly barbarous: "divide and conquer," "chip and flip," "stop and chop," "four quadrant cracking."

For years, I unthinkingly imagined cataracts growing over the outer surface of the eye. But instead they're a congealing of the lens, and the lens, of course, resides considerably *inside* the eye. It's vertically suspended in the vitreous fluid, behind the outermost shield of cornea; and behind the concentric pattern of pupil and iris and white sclera; and behind still further internal layers of muscle and tissue and membrane, all with their unique and indispensable assignments, some of them chemical, some mechanical, some a matter of elementary plumbing. It looks, the lens, like a sleek little bean, an elegant oblong of transparent tissue, and is itself a marvel of laminate fineness with it cortex and epinucleus and nucleus, expanding and flattening as it goes about its task of bending the light that passes through it and directing it, focused, to strike the retina.

Two weeks ago, I'd been thrilled to think that I would have this geezer procedure, twice, and I would see better than I ever had—*ever*. I'd begun wearing glasses, their lenses thick as pond ice, when I was five, and some sixty years later, with my cataracts removed, the world would appear to me as it never had—crisply, without the aid of glasses or contact lenses. In the matter of my sight, I'd be younger than I was when I was young. Time, *my* time, was not merely being reversed; it was going back to and beyond the place where it had started.

Now, as I waited in the same room, at the same hour, for the same reason I had waited a fortnight ago, I imagined that earlier morning as a transparent sheet being placed over this one and I sensed the two *almost* perfectly aligning. It was if I were having a *nearly* déjà vu experience. The short, round nurse who'd checked me in the first time was consulting her clipboarded records as she once again approached, and I knew when she reached me she was going to put the indicative piece of tape over my eye. And she did, this time over the right one.

Next, I knew the anesthesiologist would be coming and shortly here he was. But now the pattern of exact recurrence didn't hold. For he was not the same doctor who'd prepared me before, that sweetly ursine anesthesiologist with his black-framed glasses pushed up on his forehead, to whom I'd be forever grateful for publicly proclaiming his disbelief that I was as old as his chart told him I was. This morning, the anesthesiologist was trim and young, no black-framed glasses resting on his forehead, perched on his nose, anywhere. He greeted me and went efficiently about his tasks as I remembered them: finding a fat vein, injecting the lidocaine, clamping the oxygen tubes to my nostrils. But he made no mention of my youthful appearance. Clearly, to him I quite looked my age.

Once he was done it took little time for tranquility to again begin moving through me, and I recalled this as the moment, two weeks ago, when I'd received clear memories or dream-images of lying, a small child, in the hospital crib, sensing my mother's presence in the room, but unable to see her; and of leaving a hospital in her arms, swaddled in blankets against the cold and the snow.

But the closest I could come to re-creating that moment was to remember now what I'd remembered then.

This awareness of the two mornings, almost the same but not the same, defined them and the space of time between them distinctly—fourteen days from the entire store of days I have, consumed in the act of living them. In other words, this second surgery, after which my right eye would see as well as my left now saw, was not only a way of nearly replicating time. It was a way of measuring my time's progress toward its end.

And then, in the tall-windowed room, I felt myself moving with the anesthetic away from time's calibrations altogether. I was afloat in a place where time was not a feature, had no function. Here was the place I'd passed through on my way to unconsciousness two weeks before when the split-screen picture of my mother and me—she in her hospital bed in Iowa, I in mine here in Boston—had come to me.

The memory of that moment had returned many times these past two weeks, because it had been so powerfully convincing and so wrong. But now, this morning, though I had the same trappings of my hospital gown, my oxygen tubes, all the props and paraphernalia, there was no chance of replicating it. To do that, my mother would have had to still be alive.

Behind me was a set of swinging doors leading to the operating room. There, while they chatted and moved about preparing for the next patient, Dr. Peter Rapoza and the nurses and technicians stood with their arms folded against their chests to make sure they didn't touch anything sterile. Their poses suggested a milling band of congenial cultists, of people waiting for the start of some druidic ritual. Everyone of course wore a cap and booties and blue scrubs, and for surgical footwear Rapoza wore a pair of Crocs.

He is a tall, classically handsome man with thick silver hair, dashing in the way of beaming leading men from '30s movies, say Robert Montgomery or Richard Arlen. He's deeply convivial, though it's not a contradiction to say he's also legendarily focused and unflappable. His operating-room assistant tells a story of once having to inform him, in the middle of a surgery, that the emergency telephone call she'd just taken brought word that his house was on fire. Instruments in hand, he calmly nodded and continued.

He speaks with a baritone ebullience, which is now slightly muffled through his mask as I, anesthetized, am wheeled through the doors. The room's bright lights dim as if the feature were starting while a nurse helps Rapoza into his surgical vestments and stretches a fresh pair of sanitary gloves over his unusually long fingers. Outfitted, he settles in next to me. Another nurse with a tray of the instruments he'll need stands just behind his right shoulder as he briefly reacquaints himself with the shape and structure of my face.

In his layman's life he sees a face as you and I do, in all its singular complexity. Performing surgery, he sees his patient's face as faceless, an impersonal topography he must navigate—the peaks of long noses, the bluffs of flat ones, the bony ridgelines of prominent foreheads. In my case, the knolls of high cheekbones and the wells of deep-socketed eyes. Ideally, I suppose, he'd operate exclusively in Nebraska, the flatter the terrain the easier his navigation. But the length of his fingers and his ambidextrousness give him real advantage as he finds a spot to rest his working hand among the several skeletal bumps and dips and distances he must traverse.

A nurse swabs iodine around my eye and to keep my lids open they're secured with tiny clamps. Next, my face is covered above the mouth with a sheet, my right eye remaining necessarily exposed through a hole.

After positioning the surgical microscope suspended above my face, Rapoza asks for a blade with a diamond-shaped tip the size of a just-born's fingernail. Peering into the microscope he makes a first incision in my eye at its border where an hour hand would point to 7:30. Through this cut he inserts a bent hypodermic needle and begins to slice a nearly full circle in the membranous capsule just below my eye's outer surface, the bag that holds my streaked and smudged and spotted old lens, soon to be thrown into the ophthalmological trash.

Like all the other parts of us, our lenses grow stiff and inflexible with age and also, even more crucially, opaque. Usually this opacity is a simple central thickening, what looks like a yellowed translucent jelly bean inside the bigger bean of the lens. But a cataract might also take the form of radial spokes, or it might appear as a fine coating at the back of the lens, like frost on a car's rear window, except that the frost would be on the inside. These formations are not mutually exclusive and as a matter of fact I had hit the trifecta: both my cataracted lenses featured them all—galaxies of textures and patterns inside my eyes, a phantasmagoria of flecks and clumps and blemishes. It was a sight I would love to have seen.

Finished making his near-circular cut in my eye's capsular bag, Rapoza now uses the tip of his needle to move the resulting flap aside, as one would turn a page, giving him direct access to my lens. He continues, with various implements, to further loosen and structurally weaken it and it cooperates nicely. The most troublesome lenses to remove are from children's eyes, where they adhere too firmly to the tissue that surrounds them, and from those of the very elderly, whose lenses are rock hard and terribly difficult to chip away and the surgeon's work becomes a miner's. In the context of things, my cataracts are "young," and where else can you be sixty-two and not be considered too old? You can have cataract surgery. You can run for president. That's about it.

Now Rapoza makes a second incision, a tiny slit, where the hour hand would point to 10:00, then passes the ultrasonic pneumatic drill / vacuum cleaner through, its tip fitting so snugly into the incision it makes a seal. In the literature, these next stages are again described in language that makes the procedure sound like a construction worker's how-to guide. I read of sculpting a trench, of digging a trough. Of plunging a chopper deep into the nucleus. Of embedding a tip with a single burst of power. Of "wound burn" if the tip of the pneumatic drill gets too hot.

But Rapoza's hands as he works inside my eye give quite a contrary impression. They're making graceful, barely perceptible, coordinated motions. It's as if he were darning with impossible delicacy; as if he were knitting a sweater for a hummingbird. As a boy, unwittingly practicing for his future, he loved to construct intricate wooden ships in bottles, none of their countless parts larger than a matchstick.

Leaning over me and looking down into the microscope, he uses foot pedals to control the action of the pneumatic drill / vacuum cleaner tip—the speed at which it's oscillating, the length of its strokes, the strength of its suction. When, now Crocs-less in his stocking feet, he presses the pedal for more power, the ultrasound machine signals the stronger flow with a sound like a calliope, an abrupt and intermittent lilt, a carnival tune composed by John Cage. Simultaneously, he's using another pedal to control the position of the microscope, and with his left hand he's frequently spritzing some saline solution into my eye.

Once he's suctioned out all the broken bits of my old lens, Rapoza uses a forceps to grip the new one, made of silicon and folded in half like a soft taco. Then he eases it through the tiny slit—a model-ship part passing through its bottle's neck—and into my excavated capsular bag. He turns the forceps and releases the lens to let it unfold and it floats down and settles fully opened at the back of the capsule.

"Everything went beautifully," I heard him say to me as I was being wheeled out of the operating room. Ocular science and his talent and supremely refined tools had erased my more than half a century of severe myopia in thirteen minutes. And this happens as many as twenty times over the course of a normal day in Rapoza's operating room. Stunningly improved eyesight as a kind of delicately fashioned widget coming off an assembly line.

His words were the first thing I took in even semi-coherently as I emerged. For the brief time of the procedure, I had sensed myself lying on my bed in the center of a small huddle, in a world of surfaces and moving bodies, while bits of talk moved, motes of language, in the air. But the surgery had proceeded "beautifully" to its conclusion while I lay in a lovely limbo, sensing that I was waiting for it to start. And the way I knew it had started was by hearing him tell me it was finished. Was it mere coincidence that I was rising to the surface of regained consciousness just in time to hear Rapoza's words? Or was something instinctive telling me, as I lay there, that it was time to come back up and rejoin my life?

The drugs had heightened certain sensory details—the murmuring voices; the sheet, with its eyehole, that made a sound I mistakenly heard as a plastic tarp's stiff crinkling; the chill of the air of the operating room and the solidity and heat of the bodies working in it. But they'd kept me dumb to the big event. It was as if I were in a dream composed of incidental flashes that didn't quite order themselves as narrative. Like the rustling of the sheets in the darkness of the infants' ward. Like the furling of the blanket protecting my head from falling snow.

But brief as the surgery was, strong as was the drug-induced illusion that no time passed, it goes without saying that it did take time. You can hear that sentence saying that it, the surgery, absconded with time, in the way that all the events of our days are thieves of a kind, taking our time. Or you can hear it describing something conscientious. The surgery took *its* time: aware of the importance of what was being timed, it drew from its own allocation and used it responsibly. Or that it took its own *sweet* time, as though surgery's time were more desirable than mine. And on and on you could go. In the course of this magical transformation of my eyesight, time had been reversed and time had been suspended and time had emphasized how mercilessly it proceeds.

In the course of my informal research, I was particularly fascinated to learn of a doctor in Boston who works obsessively to reduce the time he takes to perform this surgery. He studies tapes of himself operating, looking for God knows what that might trim a few more seconds. He stands a long measuring stick next to every supine patient to make sure the bed is adjusted to a never-varying distance from the patient's nose to the operating-room floor. He directs the nurses and assistants to position themselves for each surgery in the same exactly designated spots. He has reportedly gotten his time down to four or five minutes and performs as many as forty cataract surgeries a day.

The doctor who described this fanaticism to me argued that his colleague's motive was not greed, just a need to compete against himself that had gotten, I would say, way out of hand. I was told that the man is a fine surgeon and that his scores of patients are perfectly safe in his care. All the same, I was glad I'd been in Rapoza's, in whose operating room thirteen minutes is quite fast enough. And where everything goes beautifully, in tune with time, as it waits and repeats, as it pauses and proceeds.

Perhaps I was particularly fascinated by the story of the surgeon's relentless efforts to lower his time because it reminded me of the games I played as a boy on our farm. I was eight years old when my brother, my only sibling, was born. So, to populate my childhood and entertain myself and imagine that I was gloriously the hawk-eyed athlete I was not, I fantasized bizarre sporting events played in crowded stadiums. Any activity could become a game; any patch of grass, any front porch, any garage or machine shed a packed arena. Our dark, low-ceilinged chicken coop, for instance, where my hated chore of gathering the eggs became every afternoon a vast stadium hosting a daily televised

World Cup. How many eggs could I collect, how quickly? Could I better the world-record time I'd set the day before? I hurried with my bucket along the rows of cubbyholes, reaching in for the eggs, grabbing the nesting hens I was terrified of by the neck and, as they fiercely pecked my hand, flinging them to the floor, my goggles-thick eyeglasses fogging up with dust and sweat, while my voice in the person of the play-by-play announcer breathlessly described my masterful neck grip, my matchless technique, the likes of which would not be seen again in professional Egg Gathering any time soon.

My solitary days were filled with such events. The U.S. Gravel Road Bicycle Time Trials. The Greater Midwest Corn Row Sprint Championships. And could the cataract surgeon, with his tapes and measuring stick and exactly positioned assistants, be imagining his world all that differently as he pursues his skewed notion of Personal Best?

I picture young Peter Rapoza happily lost in the exacting privacy of his model ship building, he and his manual dexterity and his preternatural patience matched against the challenging dimensions of very tiny pieces and very tiny spaces. I, on the other hand, was lost in quite another way of play, imagining myself every day stunningly triumphant before an audience of thousands—emerging blinking and victorious from the dark of the chicken coop; or staggering out into the sunlight from high corn rows, the other contestants still back there somewhere in the field; or leaving the rest of the cyclists in my gravel dust. Winning contest after contest against time, which takes its defeats with patience and grace as it waits for the day it will start to win and, once it does, never lose again.

IOWA AND THE MIDWEST EXPERIENCE

On Behalf of the Family Farm:
Iowa Farm Women's Activism since 1945
by Jenny Barker Devine

What Happens Next? Matters of Life and Death
by Douglas Bauer

The Lost Region: Toward a Revival of Midwestern History
by Jon K. Lauck

Iowa Past to Present: The People and the Prairie,
Revised Third Edition
by Dorothy Schwieder, Thomas Morain, and Lynn Nielsen

Necessary Courage:
Iowa's Underground Railroad in the Struggle against Slavery
by Lowell J. Soike

Main Street Public Library: Community Places and Reading
Spaces in the Rural Heartland, 1876–1956
by Wayne A. Wiegand